THE ANNOTATED LUTHER STUDY EDITION

# The Bondage of the Will

## 1525

THE ANNOTATED LUTHER STUDY EDITION

# The Bondage of the Will

## 1525

VOLKER LEPPIN

**Kirsi I. Stjerna**
EDITOR

Fortress Press
Minneapolis

*Bondage of the Will, 1525*
THE ANNOTATED LUTHER STUDY EDITION

Excerpted from The Annotated Luther, Volume 2, *Word and Faith* (Minneapolis: Fortress Press, 2015), Kirsi I. Stjerna, volume editor.

Fortress Press Publication Staff:
Scott Tunseth, Project Editor
Marissa Wold Uhrina, Production Manager
Laurie Ingram, Cover Design
Esther Diley, Permissions

Copyeditor: David Lott
Series design and typesetting: Ann Delgehausen, Trio Bookworks
Proofreader: Laura Weller

Library of Congress Cataloging-in-Publication Data is available

Print ISBN: 978-1-5064-1345-7
eISBN: 978-1-5064-1346-4

The paper used in this publication meets the minimum requirements of American National Standard for Information Sciences—Permanence of Paper for Printed Library Materials, ANSI Z329, 48-1984.

Manufactured in the U.S.A.

# Contents

# Publisher's Note

## About the Annotated Luther Study Edition

The volumes in the Annotated Luther Study Edition series have first been published in one of the comprehensive volumes of The Annotated Luther series. A description of that series and the volumes can be found in the Series Introduction (p. vii). While each comprehensive Annotated Luther volume can easily be used in classroom settings, we also recognize that treatises are often assigned individually for reading and study. To facilitate classroom and group use, we have pulled key treatises along with their introductions, annotations, and images directly from the Annotated Luther Series volumes.

Please note that the study edition page numbers match the page numbers of the larger Annotated Luther volume in which it first appeared. We have intentionally retained the same page numbering to facilitate use of the study editions and larger volumes side by side.

*The Bondage of the Will, 1525,*
was first published in The Annotated Luther series,
volume 2, *Word and Faith* (2015).

# Series Introduction

## Engaging the Essential Luther

Even after five hundred years Martin Luther continues to engage and challenge each new generation of scholars and believers alike. With 2017 marking the five-hundredth anniversary of Luther's *95 Theses*, Luther's theology and legacy are being explored around the world with new questions and methods and by diverse voices. His thought invites ongoing examination, his writings are a staple in classrooms and pulpits, and he speaks to an expanding assortment of conversation partners who use different languages and hale from different geographical and social contexts.

The six volumes of The Annotated Luther edition offer a flexible tool for the global reader of Luther, making many of his most important writings available in the *lingua franca* of our times as one way of facilitating interest in the Wittenberg reformer. They feature new introductions, annotations, revised translations, and textual notes, as well as visual enhancements (illustrations, art, photos, maps, and timelines). The Annotated Luther edition embodies Luther's own cherished principles of communication. Theological writing, like preaching, needs to reflect human beings' lived experience, benefits from up-to-date scholarship, and should be easily accessible to all. These volumes are designed to help teachers and students, pastors and laypersons, and other professionals in ministry understand the context in which the documents were written, recognize how the documents have shaped Protestant and Lutheran thinking, and interpret the meaning of these documents for faith and life today.

## The Rationale for This Edition

For any reader of Luther, the sheer number of his works presents a challenge. Well over one hundred volumes comprise the scholarly edition of Luther's works, the so-called Weimar Ausgabe (WA), a publishing enterprise begun in 1883 and only completed in the twenty-first century. From 1955 to 1986, fifty-five volumes came to make up *Luther's Works* (American Edition) (LW), to which Concordia Publishing House, St. Louis, is adding still more. This English-language contribution to Luther studies, matched by similar translation projects for Erasmus of Rotterdam and John Calvin, provides a theological and historical gold mine for those interested in studying Luther's thought. But even these volumes are not always easy to use and are hardly portable. Electronic forms have increased availability, but preserving Luther in book form and providing readers with manageable selections are also important goals.

Moreover, since the publication of the WA and the first fifty-five volumes of the LW, research on the Reformation in general and on Martin Luther in particular has broken new ground and evolved, as has knowledge regarding the languages in which Luther wrote. Up-to-date information from a variety of sources is brought together in The Annotated Luther, building on the work done by previous generations of scholars. The language and phrasing of the translations have also been updated to reflect modern English usage. While the WA and, in a derivative way, LW remain the central source for Luther scholarship, the present critical and annotated English translation facilitates research internationally and invites a new generation of readers for whom Latin and German might prove an unsurpassable obstacle to accessing Luther. The WA provides the basic Luther texts (with some exceptions); the LW provides the basis for almost all translations.

## Defining the "Essential Luther"

Deciding which works to include in this collection was not easy. Criteria included giving attention to Luther's initial key works; considering which publications had the most impact in his day and later; and taking account of Luther's own favorites, texts addressing specific issues of continued importance for today, and Luther's exegetical works. Taken as a whole, these works present the many sides of Luther, as reformer, pastor, biblical interpreter, and theologian. To serve today's readers and by using categories similar to those found in volumes 31–47 of Luther's works (published by Fortress Press), the volumes offer in the main a thematic rather than strictly chronological approach to Luther's writings. The volumes in the series include:

> Volume 1: *The Roots of Reform* (Timothy J. Wengert, editor)
> Volume 2: *Word and Faith* (Kirsi I. Stjerna, editor)
> Volume 3: *Church and Sacraments* (Paul W. Robinson, editor)
> Volume 4: *Pastoral Writings* (Mary Jane Haemig, editor)
> Volume 5: *Christian Life in the World* (Hans J. Hillerbrand, editor)
> Volume 6: *The Interpretation of Scripture* (Euan K. Cameron, editor)

## The History of the Project

In 2011 Fortress Press convened an advisory board to explore the promise and parameters of a new English edition of Luther's essential works. Board members Denis Janz, Robert Kolb, Peter Matheson, Christine Helmer, and Kirsi Stjerna deliberated with

Fortress Press publisher Will Bergkamp to develop a concept and identify contributors. After a review with scholars in the field, college and seminary professors, and pastors, it was concluded that a single-language edition was more desirable than dual-language volumes.

In August 2012, Hans Hillerbrand, Kirsi Stjerna, and Timothy Wengert were appointed as general editors of the series with Scott Tunseth from Fortress Press as the project editor. The general editors were tasked with determining the contents of the volumes and developing the working principles of the series. They also helped with the identification and recruitment of additional volume editors, who in turn worked with the general editors to identify volume contributors. Mastery of the languages and unique knowledge of the subject matter were key factors in identifying contributors. Most contributors are North American scholars and native English speakers, but The Annotated Luther includes among its contributors a circle of international scholars. Likewise, the series is offered for a global network of teachers and students in seminary, university, and college classes, as well as pastors, lay teachers, and adult students in congregations seeking background and depth in Lutheran theology, biblical interpretation, and Reformation history.

## Editorial Principles

The volume editors and contributors have, with few exceptions, used the translations of LW as the basis of their work, retranslating from the WA for the sake of clarity and contemporary usage. Where the LW translations have been substantively altered, explanatory notes have often been provided. More importantly, contributors have provided marginal notes to help readers understand theological and historical references. Introductions have been expanded and sharpened to reflect the very latest historical and theological research. In citing the Bible, care has been taken to reflect the German and Latin texts commonly used in the sixteenth century rather than modern editions, which often employ textual sources that were unavailable to Luther and his contemporaries.

Finally, all pieces in The Annotated Luther have been revised in the light of modern principles of inclusive language. This is not always an easy task with a historical author, but an intentional effort has been made to revise language throughout, with creativity and editorial liberties, to allow Luther's theology to speak free from unnecessary and unintended gender-exclusive language. This important principle provides an opportunity to translate accurately certain gender-neutral German and Latin expressions that Luther employed—for example, the Latin word *homo* and the German *Mensch* mean "human being," not simply "males." Using the words *man* and *men* to translate such terms would create an ambiguity not present in the original texts. The focus is on linguistic accuracy and Luther's intent. Regarding creedal formulations and trinitarian language, Luther's own expressions have been preserved, without entering the complex and important contemporary debates over language for God and the Trinity.

The 2017 anniversary of the publication of the *95 Theses* is providing an opportunity to assess the substance of Luther's role and influence in the Protestant Reformation. Revisiting Luther's essential writings not only allows reassessment of Luther's rationale and goals but also provides a new look at what Martin Luther was about and why new generations would still wish to engage him. We hope these six volumes offer a compelling invitation.

Hans J. Hillerbrand
Kirsi I. Stjerna
Timothy J. Wengert
*General Editors*

# Abbreviations

| | |
|---|---|
| ANF | *The Ante-Nicene Fathers: Translations of the Fathers down to A.D. 325.* 10 vols. Reprint, Grand Rapids: Eerdmans, 1978 |
| Ap | *Apology of the Augsburg Confession* |
| BC | *The Book of Concord*, ed. Robert Kolb and Timothy J. Wengert (Minneapolis: Fortress Press, 2000). |
| BSLK | *Die Bekenntnichriften der evngelich-lutherichen Kirche.* 11th ed. (Gottingen: Vandenhoeck & Ruprecht, 1992). |
| CA | *Augsburg Confession (Confessio Augustana)* |
| CR | *Corpus Reformatorum: Philippi Melanthonis opera quae supersunt omnia,* ed. Karl Brettschneider and Heinrich Bindseil, 28 vols. (Braunschweig: Schwetchke, 1834-1860). |
| CSEL | *Corpus Scriptorum Ecclesiasticorum Latinorum (CSEL)*, 99 vols. 1866-2011. |
| CWE | *Spirituality: Enchiridon/De contemptu mundi/Devidua christiana*, vol. 66 (University of Toronto Press, 1988), 39. |
| Ep | *Epitome of the Formula of Concord* |
| FC | *Formula of Concord* |
| LC | *Large Catechism* |
| LW | *Luther's Works* [American edition], ed. Helmut Lehmann and Jaroslav Pelikan, 55 vols. (Philadelphia: Fortress Press/St. Louis: Concordia Publishing House, 1955-1986). |
| MLStA | *Martin Luther: Studienausgabe*, ed. Hans-Ulrich Delius, 6 vols. (Berlin/Leipzig: Evangelische Verlagsanstalt, 1979-1999). |
| MPG | *Patrologiae Cursus Completus, Series Graeca*, ed. J. P. Migne, 61 vols., (Paris, 1857-1912). |
| MPL | *Patrologiae cursus completus, series Latina*, ed. Jacques-Paul Migne, 217 vols. (Paris, 1815-1875). |
| NPNF | *Nicene and Post-Nicene Fathers*, ed. Philip Schaaf and Henry Wace, series 1, 14 vols.; and series 2, 14 vols. (London/New York: T&T Clark, 1886-1900). |
| OHMLT | *The Oxford Handbook of Martin Luther's Theology*, eds. Robert Kolb, Irene Dingel, and L'ubomír Batka (New York: Oxford University Press, 2015) |
| SA | *Smalcald Articles* |
| SBOp | Sancti Bernardi Opera 3 (Rome: Editiones Cistercienses, 1963). |
| SD | *Solid Declaration of the Formula of Concord* |
| *STh* | *Summa Theologica* |
| TAL | *The Annotated Luther*, vols. 1-6 (Minneapolis: Fortress Press, 2015-2017). |
| Tr | *Treatise on the Power and Primacy of the Pope* |

| | |
|---|---|
| WA | Luther, Martin. *Luthers Werke: Kritische Gesamtausgabe* [*Schriften*], 73 vols. (Weimar: H. Böhlau, 1883–2009) |
| WA Br | Luther, Martin. *Luthers Werke: Kritische Gesamtausgabe: Briefwechsel*, 18 vols. (Weimar: H. Böhlau, 1930–1985). |
| WA DB | Luther, Martin. *Luthers Werke: Kritische Gesamtausgabe: Deutsche Bibel*, 12 vols. (Weimar: H. Böhlau, 1906–1961). |
| WA TR | Luther, Martin. *Luthers Werke: Kritische Gesamtausgabe: Tischreden*, 6 vols. (Weimar: H. Böhlau, 1912–1921). |

# The Bondage of the Will

## 1525

VOLKER LEPPIN

## INTRODUCTION

There would have been no Reformation without humanism: going back to the sources—*ad fontes!*—was the key motto of many of the humanists, and Luther's program of *sola scriptura* fitted best to it. Also, it was the *Novum Instrumentum*, Erasmus's new edition of the New Testament, that helped Luther develop his ideas while reading Paul's letter to the Romans.[1] Even more, when Melanchthon came to Wittenberg in 1518, and when Luther was admired by the humanists at the Heidelberg disputation[2] the same year, the alliance between humanism and reformation seemed to be perfect.[3]

This is true, although in Heidelberg, among other positions, Luther maintained this radical conclusion: the free will after the fall is nothing more than a name. Later on, this issue would become the point of serious contention between Erasmus of Rotterdam (1466–1536), the leader of the humanists in the north of the Alps, and Luther. Erasmus did not come into the struggle on his own, but he was strongly encouraged by others to write against Luther on the question of the free will. Concerning his planned tract, he was in contact with King Henry VIII of England (1491–1547) as well as with Pope Clement VII (1478–1534). Finally, in the beginning of September 1524, Erasmus's *De libero*

**1.** In his 1545 *Preface to the Complete Edition of Luther's Latin Writings* (LW 34:327–38), Luther recalls his reformation discovery with Romans 1:17: "Here I felt that I was altogether born again and had entered paradise itself through open gates. There a totally other face of the entire Scripture showed itself to me" (337).

**2.** Luther's "friendly" hearing with his Augustinian monks. The twenty-eight theses Luther defended at the disputation were published as the *Heidelberg Disputation* in 1518 (LW 31).

**3.** Timeline

*arbitrio diatribe sive collation* (*On the Free Will. Discourses or Comparisons*), was published.

The title indicates the two parts of his treatise: the first part was a comparison of biblical sentences relevant to the question of the free will. With this, Erasmus accepted Luther's methodological demand to discuss on biblical grounds only. But at the same time, he argued that the biblical view on this matter was not absolutely evident or decisive. He showed that different passages of the Bible argued for one or the other side of the question and thus led to possibly different answers. This observation gave Luther the justification for the discourse that ensued in the second part where he argued philosophically in a balanced manner.

The title page of Erasmus' text of the New Testament, 1516.

Portrait of Desiderius Erasmus of Rotterdam by Pilaster Hans Holbein the Younger (1498–1543).

Holding with Luther that human salvation depended fully on God, nevertheless, Erasmus stated that the human free will had survived the fall, but in a weakened mode.

When Luther read this treatise, he was horrified. It was not a surprise to him that the former collaborator did not share all his convictions. But now he was faced with something he could not accept or ignore, even if his first reaction had been to not even bother responding in public, as he wrote to Georg Spalatin[4] on 1 November 1524.[a] Just sixteen days later, Luther announced: "I will answer to Erasmus, not just because of himself, but because of those who misuse his authority for their own glory against Christ."[b] He was not the only one to distance himself from Erasmus: also the Strasburg reformers Wolfgang Capito (1478–1541), Caspar Hedio (1494–1542), and Martin Bucer (1491–1551) supported Luther in his opposition of the man they saw opening the way for the Antichrist—even if, they confessed, they had learned a lot from Erasmus.[c]

Actually, Luther had no time to answer quickly. Other problems were coming into the foreground, mainly the Peasants' Wars. Asked for his statement, Luther suddenly became engaged in a severe debate about the legitimacy of this uproar of peasants demanding their rights. Luther felt his popularity failing and feared that the war could destroy all his efforts for reforms. In addition, he got married in 1525 to Katharina von Bora (1499–1552)—an important step in his development as a man and a reformer—but also one that only further fueled his critics who jeered about the monk becoming a spouse. Luther took the whole spring of 1525 to stew on his answer against Erasmus, as his letters reveal, with several allusions to this issue,[d] but he had no time. As late as 27 September 1525, Luther wrote to Nicholaus Hausmann (c. 1478–1538):[5] "I am now fully engaged in confuting Erasmus."[e] Not long after, in December, the *De servo arbitrio* (*The Bondage of the Will*) was published.

**4.** Georg Spalatin (1484–1545) was Luther's friend and a counselor/diplomat of the Elector of Saxony.

**5.** A Lutheran preacher in Anhalt-Dessau, superintendent, and teacher—from Bavaria but with the call in Bohemia—Hausmann was interested in the worship reforms and actively corresponded with Luther.

a  WA Br 3:368, 30–31 (No. 789).

b  WA Br 3:373, 6–8 (No. 793).

c  WA Br 3:386, 207–15 (No. 797).

d  See for example WA Br 3:462, 6 (No. 847): "I must [write] against the Free will." WA Br 3:462, 6 (No. 789).

e  WA Br 3:582, 5 (No. 926).

The treatise is important on four accounts: (1) as a witness of the serious intellectual debates in the Reformation time; (2) as a contribution to the developing Lutheran teaching on the Holy Scripture; (3) on free will; and (4) on God. Concerning the culture of debate in which Luther operated, one sees Luther acting as someone who wanted to show his own humanist education. No text of his is as full of allusions to antic traditions as *De servo arbitrio* is. Luther wanted to show Erasmus and, even more, the public that he was not intellectually inferior, even if he, in a figure of humility, confessed his own limitations. And he did not hide the main difference: while Erasmus tried to open the discussion and left it to his readers to decide which position would be right, Luther impressed upon his readers that the struggle was about the truth and that it was urgent to come to the conclusion that Luther himself clearly suggested.

Luther's absolute conviction about what was right lay in his doctrine of Scripture. Against Erasmus, who had maintained that the question of free will could not be decided just on the basis of the Bible, Luther stressed the clarity imbedded in Scripture: if human beings did not understand Scripture satisfactorily, this was not the failure of Scripture but of the human reason, which was not able to understand the depth of God's truth. With these passages, Luther laid the grounds for the fundamental Lutheran understanding of the infallibility of Scripture and its centrality in Lutheran theology, especially prominent in the so-called Lutheran orthodoxy.[6]

Luther's position on the main question seems easy to summarize—and yet it is not. There is no question at all that he upheld his early conviction that human beings do not have free will. But he tried to reconcile this with the human experience, which calls on individuals to be able to decide on many things in everyday life. Luther thus stressed that his denial of the free will pertained to the issue of salvation, while in other areas of life, not relevant for this fundamental existential matter, free will could be acknowledged. Luther's conclusions have continued to stir reflection and debate among Lutherans over the centuries and continue even today. Luther's argument on the matter of bound/free will poses a challenge and an invitation for constructive contemporary theology.

The same can be said about the fourth question: Luther's doctrine of God. He introduces the distinction of the revealed

**6.** Lutheran orthodoxy refers to a period from the compilation of the 1580 *Book of Concord* to the Age of Enlightenment.

and the hidden God to make clear that a Christian must focus on God as shown in Jesus Christ rather than speculating about God's potency in general. Depending on one's own convictions, one can see this as one of Luther's deepest spiritual insights, or as a speculative idea, leading to a destruction of a consistent image of God. However, the idea is rooted in Luther's early conversations with his confessor Johann von Staupitz (c. 1460–1524),[7] who was instrumental in directing Luther's mind and attention to move from the fear of predestination[8] to trust in the Redeemer, Jesus Christ.

These basic ideas are part of a long and sometimes confusing text that Luther completed hastily. The original Latin text was addressed to the learned scholars, but soon Luther's colleague and the Wittenberg city pastor, Justus Jonas (1493–1555), provided a German translation to make it known also for the broader public. Erasmus himself was mainly disturbed with Luther's style. He criticized Luther's ferocity, idiosyncrasy, and even malice[f] and wrote his answer, *A Defense of the Diatribe* (*Hyperaspistes diatribae*), which was published in two volumes in 1526 and 1527. Again, external challenges and his inner reluctance prevented Luther from returning the favor with his new answer. Thus the debate eventually petered out between the two, while the issue did not die.

The consequences of this relatively brief public debate were immense: many humanists retreated from Luther because of his intransigent manner of debating. The coinciding Peasants' Wars made things even worse. Luther's glory failed; the former hero became a representative of intellectual headiness. Nevertheless, the text of *De servo arbitrio*, read independently from its immediate context, provides an abundance of theological insights for new generations of theologians to address the fundamental concerns about human freedom, God's omnipotence, and the premise of the God-human relationship—and thus, naturally, the question about salvation.

In the text of *The Bondage of the Will* that follows, several cuts have been made in order to provide a representative portion of the whole. The following symbol [. . .] is used to indicate where content has been edited out.

**7.** Staupitz was a university preacher, the Vicar-General of the Augustinians in Germany, and Luther's abbot and spiritual father who had a significant influence on his theology of grace. See Franz Posset, *The Front-Runner of the Catholic Reformation: The Life and Works of Johann von Staupitz* (Farnham, UK: Ashgate, 2003).

**8.** The concept of predestination, rooted in Romans 9–11, was shaped by Augustine. To him, all human beings formed a mass of perdition after the fall. But with divine incomprehensible volition, God decided to save some of them by no reason than God's good will alone, which on the other hand meant there was no other reason why the other human beings should not be preserved.

*f*  WA 18:583.

**9.** This translation is based on the translation provided by Philip S. Watson, in collaboration with Benjamin Drewery, in *Luther's Works*, vol. 33: *Career of the Reformer III*, ed. Jaroslav J. Pelikan, Hilton C. Oswald, and Helmut T. Lehmann (Philadelphia: Fortress Press, 1972), 3–295. Revised by Volker Leppin according to the principles of *The Annotated Luther*, with a new introduction and enhanced annotations. The Latin text of *De servo arbitrio* used is from WA 18:600–787 and MLStA 3:177–356. The latter provided important support for annotation.

**10.** Luther here does not call Erasmus a "master" in the technical sense of an academic graduate.

**11.** Being concerned with the Peasants' Wars (1525), it took Luther about one year to answer Erasmus's *Diatribe*, which was published in September 1524. Luther's *De servo arbitrio* was published in December 1525.

**12.** The Maccabees were the leaders of Jewish revolt against the Hellenist ruler Antiochus Epiphanes IV in the second century before Christ.

# THE BONDAGE OF THE WILL[9]

TO THE VENERABLE MASTER[10] ERASMUS of Rotterdam, Martin Luther sends grace and peace in Christ.

## [Introduction]

### [Luther Explains His Delay in Replying and Admits Erasmus's Superior Talent]

That I have taken so long[11] to reply to your *Diatribe Concerning Free Choice*, venerable Erasmus, has been contrary to everyone's expectation and to my own custom; for until now I have seemed not only willing to accept, but eager to seek out, opportunities of this kind for writing. There will perhaps be some surprise at this new and unwonted forbearance—or fear!—in Luther, who has not been roused even by all the speeches and letters his adversaries have flung about, congratulating Erasmus on his victory and chanting in triumph, "Ho, ho! Has that Maccabee,[12] that most obstinate Assertor,[13] at last met his match, and dares not open his mouth against him?" Yet not only do I not blame them, but of myself I yield you a palm such as I have never yielded to anyone before; for I confess not only that you are far superior to me in powers of eloquence and native genius (which we all must admit, all the more as I am a barbarian who has always lived among barbarians[14]), but that you have quite damped my spirit and eagerness, and left me exhausted before I could strike a blow.

There are two reasons for this: first, your virtuosity in treating the subject with such remarkable and consistent moderation as to make it impossible for me to be angry with you; and second, the luck or chance or fate by which you say nothing on this important subject that has not been said before.[15] Indeed, you say so much less, and attribute so much more to free choice than the Sophists[16] have hitherto done (a point on which I shall have more to say later) that it really seemed superfluous to answer the arguments you use. They have been refuted already so often by me, and beaten down and completely pulverized in Philip Melanchthon's *Loci Communes* [*Commonplaces*][17]—an unanswerable little book, which in my judgment deserves not only to be honored with immortality but also with ecclesiastical authority.

# LOCI

### COMMVNES RERVM.
### THEOLOGICARVM
### SEV HYPOTY,
### POSES THEO,
### LOGICAE.

### VVITTEMBERGAE.
### AN. M. D. XXI.

The title page of Philip Melanchthon's
*Loci communes rerum theologicarum, seu,
Hypotyposes theologicae*, a volume that later
proved to be the first Protestant attempt
at systematic theology.

**13.** In his *Assertio omnium articulorum Martini Lutheri per bullam Leonis X novissimam Damnatorum*, Luther had asserted his articles that had been damned in the bull *Exsurge Domine* by Pope Leo X (1475–1521).

**14.** Actually, Luther had enjoyed a good humanist education in Erfurt, but his Latin was far worse than Erasmus's was, even if he tried to show his good abilities in this tract. This may be a possible allusion to Erasmus's book *Against the Barbarians* (1520). For Erasmus the "barbarians" were those who opposed *bonae literae* or "good letters" (LW 33:15).

**15.** Allusion to the Prologue in Terence's comedy *Eunuchus*: "Nothing is said now, that was not said before."

**16.** Sophists were the counterparts of Socrates in Plato's dialogues, always blamed to twist everybody's words. In Luther's use, the word *sophists* was an overall invective against the Scholastics.

**17.** Melanchthon's *Loci communes*, written in 1521, was the first systematic dogmatic treatise in the Wittenberg Reformation. In *Loci*, most important concepts of the Bible, as structural elements of the dogmatics, meant a change from the Scholastic kind of systematic dialectical structuring.

**18.** Obviously, Luther, as a humanistically trained teacher, uses here the argument of distinguishing the fine humanist form from unimportant matters.

**19.** This, indeed, was Luther's impression of Erasmus's *Diatribe* from his first view on, as revealed in his letter to Spalatin from the 1 November 1524, where he argues against the *Diatribe* as an "unlearned book of such a learned man" (WA Br 3:368, 30–31 [No. 789]).

**20.** Luther was convinced, in light of Rom. 1:18-21, that every person's conscience was confronted with God and able to hear God's will.

**21.** Passages like this, later on, could give rise to the hermeneutics that made a sharp distinction between the letters of Scripture and a spiritual interpretation of it. Luther himself was convinced that the Spirit was connected with the Scripture and its letters.

Compared with it, your book struck me as so cheap and trivial that I felt profoundly sorry for you, defiling as you were your very elegant and ingenious style with such trash,[18] and quite disgusted at the utterly unworthy matter that was being conveyed in such rich ornaments of eloquence, like refuse or ordure being carried in gold and silver vases.[19]

You seem to have felt this yourself, from the reluctance with which you undertook this piece of writing. No doubt your conscience warned you that[20] no matter what powers of eloquence you brought to the task, you would be unable so to gloss it over as to prevent me from stripping away the seductive charm of your words and discovering the dregs beneath, since although I am unskilled in speech, I am not unskilled in knowledge, by the grace of God. For, in full faith, I venture thus with Paul [1 Cor. 11:6] to claim knowledge for myself that I deny to you, though I grant you eloquence and native genius such as I willingly and very properly disclaim for myself.

What I thought, then, was this. If there are those who have imbibed so little of our teaching or taken so insecure a hold of it, strongly supported by Scripture though it is, that they can be moved by these trivial and worthless though highly decorative arguments of Erasmus, then they do not deserve that I should come to their rescue with an answer. Nothing could be said or written that would be sufficient for such people, even though it were by recourse to thousands of books a thousand times over, and you might just as well plow the seashore and sow seed in the sand[g] or try to fill a cask full of holes with water.[h] Those who have imbibed the Spirit who holds sway in our books have had a sufficient service from us already, and they can easily dispose of your performances; but as for those who read without the Spirit,[21] it is no wonder if they are shaken like a reed by every wind.[i] Why, even God could not say enough for such people, even if all God's creatures were turned into tongues. Hence I might well have decided to leave them alone, upset as they were by your book, along with those who are delighted with it and declare you the victor.

It was, then, neither pressure of work, nor the difficulty of the task, nor your great eloquence, nor any fear of you, but sheer dis-

g    Allusion to Ovid, *Heroides* 5, 115.
h    Allusion to Plautus, *Pseudolus* 269.
i     Cf. Matt. 11:7.

gust, anger, and contempt, or—to put it plainly—my considered judgment on your *Diatribe* that damped my eagerness to answer you. I need hardly mention here the good care you take, as you always do, to be everywhere evasive and equivocal;[22] you fancy yourself steering more cautiously than Ulysses between Scylla and Charybdis as you seek to assert nothing while appearing to assert something.[23] How, I ask you, is it possible to have any discussion or reach any understanding with such people unless one is clever enough to catch Proteus?[24] What I can do in this matter, and what you have gained by it, I will show you later, with Christ's help.

There have, then, to be special reasons for my answering you at this point. Faithful Christians are urging me to do so, and point out that everyone expects it, since the authority of Erasmus is not to be despised, and the truth of Christian doctrine is being imperiled in the hearts of many. Moreover, it has at length come home to me that my silence has not been entirely honorable, and that I have been deluded by my mundane prudence—or malice—into insufficient awareness of my duty, whereby I am under obligation both to the wise and to the foolish [Rom. 1:14], especially when I am called to it by the entreaties of so many Christians. For although the subject before us demands more than an external scholar, and besides him who plants and him who waters outwardly [1 Cor. 3:7], it requires also the Spirit of God to give the growth and to teach living things inwardly (a thought that has been much in my mind), yet since the Spirit is free, and blows not where we will but where he wills [John 3:8], we ought to have observed that rule of Paul, "Be urgent in season and out of season" [2 Tim. 4:2], for we do not know at what hour the Lord is coming [Matt. 24:42]. There may be, I grant, some who have not yet sensed the Spirit who informs my writings, and who have been bowled over by that *Diatribe* of yours; perhaps their hour has not yet come.[25]

And who knows but that God may even deign to visit you, excellent Erasmus, through such a wretched and frail little vessel[j] as myself, so that in a happy hour—and for this I earnestly beseech the Father of mercies[26] through Christ our Lord—I may come to you by means of this book, and win a very dear brother.

**22.** Equivocal terms in medieval theory of language meant terms with the same spelling and sound but different meanings.

**23.** Scylla and Charybdis were two monsters in antic tales, sitting opposite to one another in a strait, the first devouring human beings, the second dumping them in a swirl. Ulysses had to pass them and lost many of his companions.

**24.** Proteus was a sea goddess in antic tales, one able to transform himself into different shapes and so able to escape all who wanted to catch him.

**25.** Luther himself felt he was in the last days of the world, awaiting the imminent coming of the Lord.

**26.** *Pater misericordiae* (Lat.), "father of mercies"; this traditional expression could be translated as "parent of mercies" to express God's merciful relating to human beings in need of divine parental love.

*j*   Cf. 2 Cor. 4:7.

For although you think and write wrongly about free choice,[k] yet I owe you no small thanks, for you have made me far more sure of my own position by letting me see the case for free choice put forward with all the energy of so distinguished and powerful a mind, but with no other effect than to make things worse than before. That is plain evidence that free choice is a pure fiction;[27] for, like the woman in the Gospel [Mark 5:25f.], the more it is treated by the doctors, the worse it gets. I shall therefore abundantly pay my debt of thanks to you, if through me you become better informed, as I through you have been more strongly confirmed. But both of these things are gifts of the Spirit, not our own achievement. Therefore, we must pray that God may open my mouth and your heart, and the hearts of all human beings, and that God may be present in our midst as the master who informs both our speaking and hearing.

But from you, my dear Erasmus, let me obtain this request, that just as I bear with your ignorance in these matters, so you in turn will bear with my lack of eloquence. God does not give all his gifts to one man, and "we cannot all do all things"; or, as Paul says: "There are varieties of gifts, but the same Spirit" [1 Cor. 12:4]. It remains, therefore, for us to render mutual service with our gifts, so that each with one's own gift bears the burden and need of the other. Thus we shall fulfill the law of Christ [Gal. 6:2].[28]

# [Part I. Review of Erasmus's Preface]

## [Christianity Involves Assertions; Christians Are No Skeptics]

I want to begin by referring to some passages in your Preface, in which you rather disparage our case and puff up your own. I note, first, that just as in other books you censure me for obstinate assertiveness, so in this book you say that you are so far from delighting in assertions that you would readily take refuge in the opinion of the Skeptics[29] wherever this is allowed by the

---

**27.** Luther had stated this as early as in his 1518 *Heidelberg Disputation* (WA 1:353–74; LW 31:[37–38] 39–70). Here he explains the free will to be just a word, not a real thing (*res de solo titulo*).

**28.** As evident with the biblical and traditional wording, Luther does not find the law just in the Old but also in the New Testament.

**29.** The Skeptics in antiquity denied the possibility of finding the absolute truth. Augustine (354–430), in his *Contra academicos*, gave severe criticism of skepticism.

k    In Latin, there is a difference between *voluntas*, which means "will" as a power in terms of psychology, and *arbitrium*, which stresses the ability to choose. Luther and Erasmus address mainly the latter.

inviolable authority of the Holy Scriptures and the decrees of the Church, to which you always willingly submit your personal feelings,[30] whether you grasp what it prescribes or not. This [you say] is the frame of mind that pleases you.

I take it (as it is only fair to do) that you say these things in a kindly and peace-loving mind. But if anyone else were to say them, I should probably go for that person in my usual manner; and I ought not to allow even you, excellent though your intentions are, to be led astray by this idea. For it is not the mark of a Christian mind to take no delight in assertions; on the contrary, a human being must delight in assertions to be a real Christian. And by assertion—in order that we may not be misled by words—I mean a constant adhering, affirming, confessing, maintaining, and an invincible persevering;[31] nor, I think, does the word mean anything else either as used by the Latins[32] or by us in our time.

I am speaking, moreover, about the assertion of those things that have been divinely transmitted to us in the sacred writings. Elsewhere we have no need either of Erasmus or any other instructor to teach us that in matters that are doubtful or useless and unnecessary, assertions, disputings, and quarreling are not only foolish but impious, and Paul condemns them in more than one place.[l] Nor are you, I think, speaking of such things in this place—unless, in the manner of some foolish orator, you have chosen to announce one topic and discuss another, like the man with the turbot,[33] or else, with the craziness of some ungodly writer, you are contending that the article about free choice is doubtful or unnecessary.

Let Skeptics and Academics[34] keep well away from us Christians, but let there be among us "assertors" twice as unyielding as the Stoics themselves.[35] How often, I ask you, does the apostle Paul demand that *plerophoria* (as he terms it)[m]—that most sure and unyielding assertion of conscience? In Romans 10[:10] he calls it "confession," saying, "with the mouth confession is made unto salvation." And Christ says, "Everyone who confesses me before people, I also will confess before my Father" [Matt. 10:32]. Peter bids us give a reason for the hope that is in us [1 Peter 3:15]. What need is there to dwell on this?

**30.** Indeed, Erasmus, in his *Diatribe*, had confessed his willingness to submit his sense to the Holy Scriptures and the decrees of the church.

**31.** These remarks, however, from the beginning on show the different approaches Luther and Erasmus had regarding the dispute: while Erasmus sees the question of free will as a matter of discussion, Luther is convinced that he has already found the unquestionable truth in in the Bible.

**32.** Luther refers to the Latin authors from antiquity as examples for modern humanists.

**33.** This figure of speech derives from Juvenal's fourth *Satire*, 65–150. Luther jokes about orators who do not see or understand the issue of their speech exactly.

**34.** The Academics were the followers of Plato in antiquity. Cicero had presented them as skeptics. From this stemmed Augustine's criticism against them.

**35.** The Stoics, the most important philosophical school in antiquity, maintained that the whole cosmos is dominated by the godly *logos* (reason/word).

---

*l*  Cf. 1 Tim. 1:6; 2 Tim. 2:23; Titus 1:10; 3:9.

*m*  Cf. 1 Thess. 1:5.

Nothing is better known or more common among Christians than assertion. Take away assertions and you take away Christianity. Why, the Holy Spirit is given them from heaven to glorify Christ [in them] and confess him even unto death—unless it is not asserting when one dies for one's confession and assertion. Moreover, the Spirit goes to such lengths in asserting that she takes the initiative and accuses the world of sin [John 16:8], as if she would provoke a fight; and Paul commands Timothy to "exhort" and "be urgent out of season" [2 Tim. 4:2]. But what a droll exhorter he would be, who himself neither firmly believed nor consistently asserted the thing he was exhorting about! Why, I would send him to Anticyra![36]

But it is I who am the biggest fool, for wasting words and time on something that is clearer than daylight. What Christian would agree that assertions are to be despised? That would be nothing but a denial of all religion and piety, or an assertion that neither religion, nor piety, nor any dogma is of the slightest importance. Why, then, do you too assert, "I take no delight in assertions," and that you prefer this frame of mind to its opposite?[37] [ . . . ]

### [The Clarity of Scripture]

I come now to the second passage, which is of a piece with this. Here you distinguish between Christian dogmas, pretending that there are some which it is necessary to know, and some which it is not, and you say that some are [meant to be] obscure and others quite plain. You thus either play games with other human beings' words or else you are trying your hand at a rhetorical sally of your own. You adduce, however, in support of your views, Paul's saying in Romans 11[:33]: "Oh the depth of the riches and wisdom and knowledge of God," and also that of Isaiah 40[:13]: "Who has directed the Spirit of the Lord, or what counselor has provided instruction?"

It was easy for you to say these things, since you either knew you were not writing to Luther, but for the general public, or you did not reflect that it was Luther you were writing against, whom I hope you allow nonetheless to have some acquaintance with the Holy Scriptures and some judgment in respect of it. If you do not allow this, then I shall force you to it. The distinction I make—in order that I, too, may display a little rhetoric or

**36.** In Anticyra, hellebore was produced as a medicine against insanity (cf. Erasmus, *Adagia* 1,8,52). Luther means therefore that one should go to Anticyra to become cured from one's insanity.

**37.** With this rhetorical question, Luther suggests that Erasmus writes without any religious intention.

dialectic[38]—is this: God and the Scripture of God are two things, no less than the Creator and the creature are two things.

That in God there are many things hidden, of which we are ignorant, no one doubts—as the Lord himself says concerning the last day: "Of that day no one knows but the Father" [Mark 13:32], and in Acts 1[:7]: "It is not for you to know times and seasons"; and again: "I know whom I have chosen" [John 13:18], and Paul says: "The Lord knows those who are his" [2 Tim. 2:19], and so forth. But that in Scripture there are some things abstruse, and everything is not plain—this is an idea put about by the ungodly Sophists, with whose lips you also speak here, Erasmus; but they have never produced, nor can they produce, a single article to prove this mad notion of theirs. Yet with such a phantasmagoria[39] Satan has frightened people away from reading the sacred writings and has made Holy Scripture contemptible, in order to enable the plagues it has bred from philosophy to prevail in the Church.[40]

I admit, of course, that there are many texts in the Scriptures that are obscure and abstruse, not because of the majesty of their subject matter, but because of our ignorance of their vocabulary and grammar; but these texts in no way hinder a knowledge of all the subject matter of Scripture. For what still more sublime thing can remain hidden in the Scriptures, now that the seals have been broken, the stone rolled from the door of the sepulcher [Matt. 27:66; 28:2], and the supreme mystery brought to light, namely, that Christ the Son of God has been made man, that God is three and one,[41] that Christ has suffered for us and is to reign eternally? Are not these things known and sung even in the highways and byways? Take Christ out of the Scriptures, and what will you find left in them?[42]

The subject matter of the Scriptures, therefore, is all quite accessible, even though some texts are still obscure owing to our ignorance of their terms. Truly it is stupid and impious, when we know that the subject matter of Scripture has all been placed in the clearest light, to call it obscure on account of a few obscure words. If the words are obscure in one place, yet they are plain in another; and it is one and the same theme, published quite openly to the whole world, which in the Scriptures is sometimes expressed in plain words, and sometimes lies as yet hidden in obscure words. Now, when the item is in the light, it does not matter if this or that sign of it is in darkness,[43] since many other

38. Together with grammar, rhetoric and dialectics were parts of the studies of arts in the Middle Ages, together framing the so-called *Trivium*.

39. A delusion, a picture in a dream.

40. Luther's main argument against the Scholastics consists of criticism of their theology and philosophy. In general, Luther does not deny the means of philosophy but its use in theology. It is a kind of human wisdom, while theology has to deal with divine insights.

41. For Luther, the Trinity was clearly witnessed in the Holy Scriptures, which he read, in this regard, through the lenses of the ecumenical creeds' trinitarian formulation.

42. From his first lectures on the Bible (on Psalms and Romans) in the years 1513–1516, Luther was convinced about Christ being at the core of Scripture.

43. Luther here alludes to the famous distinction Augustine made between item/matter (*res*) and sign (*signum*) to interpret the sacraments, and widely used in the Middle Ages for that purpose.

signs of the same thing are meanwhile in the light. Who will say that a public fountain is not in the light because those who are in a narrow side street do not see it, whereas all who are in the marketplace do see it?

Your reference to the Corycian cave,[44] therefore, is irrelevant; that is not how things are in the Scriptures. Matters of the highest majesty and the profoundest mysteries are no longer hidden away, but have been brought out and are openly displayed before the very doors. For Christ has opened our minds so that we may understand the Scriptures [Luke 24:45], and the gospel is preached to the whole creation [Mark 16:15]; "Their voice has gone out to all the earth" [Rom. 10:18], and "Whatever was written was written for our instruction" [Rom. 15:4]; also: "All Scripture inspired by God is profitable for teaching" [1 Tim. 3:16]. See, then, whether you and all the Sophists[45] can produce any single mystery that is still abstruse in the Scriptures.

It is true that for many people much remains abstruse; but this is not due to the obscurity of Scripture, but to the blindness or indolence of those who will not take the trouble to look at the very clearest truth. [...]

To put it briefly, there are two kinds of clarity in Scripture, just as there are also two kinds of obscurity: one external and pertaining to the ministry of the Word,[46] the other located in the understanding of the heart. If you speak of the internal clarity, no human being perceives one iota of what is in the Scriptures unless he has the Spirit of God. All human beings have a darkened heart,[47] so that even if they can recite everything in Scripture, and know how to quote it, yet they apprehend and truly understand nothing of it. They neither believe in God, nor that they themselves are creatures of God, nor anything else, as Ps. 13[14:1] says: "The fool has said in his heart, 'There is no god.'"[48] For the Spirit is required for the understanding of Scripture, both as a whole and in any part of it.[49] If, on the other hand, you speak of the external clarity, nothing at all is left obscure or ambiguous, but everything there is in the Scriptures has been brought out by the Word into the most definite light and published to all the world.

---

**44.** Erasmus compared human knowledge of God with the antic knowledge of this cave near Tarsus with many hallways.

**45.** See n. 16, p. 159.

**46.** Referring to the public preaching.

**47.** Luther here describes the situation of human beings after the fall, stressing their loss of all good powers.

**48.** This verse was very famous in medieval theological literature: Anselm of Canterbury (1033–1109) used it to show the possibility of human beings denying God's existence. Against this attitude, he wrote his *Proslogion*, demonstrating God's existence.

### [It Is Vital to Know the Truth about Free Choice]

But what is still more intolerable is that you count this subject of free choice among the things that are useless and unnecessary, and replace it for us with a list of the things you consider sufficient for the Christian devotion. It is such a list as any Jew or Gentile totally ignorant of Christ could certainly draw up with ease, for you make not the slightest mention of Christ, as if you think that Christian godliness can exist without Christ

Bust of Greek philosopher Epicurus.

so long as God is worshiped with all one's powers[50] as being by nature most merciful. What am I to say here, Erasmus? You reek of nothing but Lucian,[51] and you breathe out on me the vast drunken folly of Epicurus.[52] If you consider this subject unnecessary for Christians, then please quit the field; you and I have nothing in common, for I consider it vital. [. . .]

[It] is not irreverent, inquisitive, or superfluous, but essentially salutary and necessary for a Christian, to find out whether the will does anything or nothing in matters pertaining to eternal salvation. Indeed, as you should know, this is the core issue between us, the point on which everything in this controversy

**49.** With this, Luther does not plead for a fully spiritual basis of Christian understanding. This would be *schwärmerisch* ("fanatic") to him. What he wants to show is the indispensable connection of Spirit and Scripture.

**50.** Here, Luther saw a contradiction to the teaching of justification: to him, human powers were destroyed by the fall, and since then human beings were not able to worship God perfectly nor to follow God fully.

**51.** Lucian of Samosata (c. 125–180), a Greek writing satirist of the second century, had become famous through the translation of his works into Latin by Erasmus and Thomas Morus (1478–1535) (publication of all works in 1517).

**52.** Epicurus (341–270 BCE) was a Greek philosopher who taught that pleasure is the highest good (hedonism). He did not envision pleasure in the sense of gross indulgence; rather, he valued the contentment that results from giving up desires, fears, and ambitions. But many Greek and Roman Epicureans failed to make this distinction.

**53.** Deriving from this passage, many interpreters hold that Luther's position in *De servo arbitrio* is far different from philosophical determinism, because he is only engaged in the means of free will concerning matters of salvation. Here his clear answer is: the free will has nothing to do with salvation.

**54.** It is characteristic for Luther to understand "omnipotence" in the sense of God being active and efficient in all things.

**55.** Interestingly enough, Luther here picks up the argument of Rom. 1:20 that was central for medieval Scholastic theology for the possibility to demonstrate God's existence. As early as in the *Heidelberg Disputation* in 1518, Luther had proven himself quite skeptical against arguments like this, blaming them as a special type of "theology of glory."

**56.** Five years earlier, Luther identified his tract *On the Freedom of a Christian* (1520) as the sum of the Christian life.

**57.** This sentence that speaks of "anything" and "everything" clearly indicates a philosophical determinism, a position that all things happen by (divine) necessity.

turns.[53] For what we are doing is to inquire what free choice can do, what it has done to it, and what is its relation to the grace of God. If we do not know these things, we shall know nothing at all of things Christian, and shall be worse than any heathen. Anyone who does not feel this should confess to be no Christian. Anyone who even disparages or scorns it should know that he or she is the greatest enemy of Christians. For if I am ignorant of what, how far, and how much I can and may do in relation to God, it will be equally uncertain and unknown to me, what, how far, and how much God can and may do in me, although it is God who works everything in everyone [1 Cor. 12:6].[54] But when the works and power of God are unknown, I do not know God in Godself,[55] and when God is unknown, I cannot worship, praise, thank, and serve God, since I do not know how much I ought to attribute to myself and how much to God. It therefore behooves us to be very certain about the distinction between God's power and our own, God's work and our own, if we want to live a godly life.

So you see that this problem is one-half of the whole sum[56] of Christian issues, since on it both knowledge of oneself and the knowledge and glory of God quite vitally depend. That is why we cannot permit you, my dear Erasmus, to call such knowledge irreverent, inquisitive, and vain. We owe much to you, but godliness claims our all. Why, you yourself are aware that all the good in us is to be ascribed to God, and you assert this in your description of Christianity. But in asserting this, you are surely asserting also that the mercy of God alone does everything, and that our will does nothing, but rather is passive; otherwise, all is not ascribed to God. Yet a little later you say that it is not religious, pious, and salutary to assert or to know this. But a mind compelled to talk like that is inconsistent with itself, uncertain and inexpert in matters of religion.

### [God's Foreknowledge; Contingency and Necessity]ⁿ

The other half of the Christian *summa* is concerned with knowing whether God foreknows anything contingently, and whether we do everything of necessity.[57] And this, too, you find irrever-

*n* WA 18:614–20.

ent, inquisitive, and vain, just as all ungodly people do, or rather, as the demons and the damned[o] find it hateful and detestable. You are well advised to steer clear of such questions if you can, but you are a pretty poor rhetorician and theologian when you presume to discuss and expound free choice without the two subjects just mentioned. I will act as a whetstone and, although no rhetorician myself, will teach a distinguished rhetorician his business.

Suppose Quintilian, proposing to write about oratory, were to say: "In my judgment, that stupid and superfluous stuff about choice of subject, arrangement of material, style, memorization, delivery, ought to be omitted; suffice it to know that oratory is the art of speaking well"[p]—would you not ridicule such an exponent of the art? Yet you act no differently yourself. You propose to write about free choice, and you begin by rejecting and throwing away the whole substance and all the elements of the subject on which you are going to write. For you cannot possibly know what free choice is unless you know what the human will can do, and what God does, and whether he foreknows necessarily.

Do not even your rhetoricians teach you that when you are going to speak on any subject, you ought to say first whether it exists, then what it is, what its parts are, what things are contrary to it, akin to it, similar to it, etc.? But you deprive free choice (poor thing!) of all these advantages, and lay down no question concerning it, unless perhaps the first, namely, whether it exists; and you do this with arguments (as we shall see) of such a kind that, apart from the elegance of the language, I have never seen a feebler book on free choice. The very Sophists provide at least a better discussion on this subject, for while they have no idea of style, yet when they tackle free choice they do define all the questions connected with it—whether it exists, what it is, what it does, how it is related, etc.—though even they do not succeed in doing what they set out to do. In this book, therefore, I shall press you and all the Sophists hard until you define for me the strength and effectiveness of free choice; and I shall press you

---

o   *Daemones et damnati* is not just a linguistic game, but also refers to the
    center of the question under debate: the damned are those who are not
    predestinated "positively," that is, to the salvation.

p   Quintilian, *Insitutiones oratoriae* 2,15,38.

**58.** This argument obviously excludes all freedom from creatures. While with the divine prescience, some human freedom could prevail, God's purpose and acting by the divine immutable will makes all things completely dependent on God.

**59.** This argument shows that Luther, even when he speaks in terms of a general philosophical determination, starts with the question of grace and justification.

**60.** The question of predestination for Later Scholasticism was mainly a question of the logical possibility of God's immutable foreknowledge in a world of contingencies.

**61.** Luther interprets "contingency" as virtually equivalent to "chance." Luther's debate with Erasmus on "free will" relates to the centuries of debate regarding the meaning of the words *causality* and *necessity*. Aristotle was the first to argue for indeterminism identifying the prime mover and a chain of different causes (material, efficient, formal, and final). The medieval

(with Christ's aid) so hard that I hope I shall make you repent of ever having published your *Diatribe*.

Here, then, is something fundamentally necessary and salutary for a Christian, to know that God foreknows nothing contingently, but that God foresees and purposes and does[58] all things by God's own immutable, eternal, and infallible will. Here is a thunderbolt by which free choice is completely prostrated and shattered, so that those who want free choice asserted must either deny or explain away this thunderbolt, or get rid of it by some other means. However, before I establish this point by my own argument and the authority of Scripture, I will first deal with it in your words.

Was it not you, my dear Erasmus, who asserted a little earlier that God is by nature just, by nature most merciful? If this is true, does it not follow that God is immutably just and merciful—that as God's nature never changes, so neither does God's justice or mercy? But what is said of God's justice and mercy must also be said of God's knowledge, wisdom, goodness, will, and other divine attributes.[59] If, then, the assertion of these things concerning God is, as you state, religious, pious, and salutary, what has come over you that you now contradict yourself by asserting that it is irreverent, inquisitive, and vain to say that God foreknows necessarily? You declare that the will of God is to be understood as immutable, yet you forbid us to know that God's foreknowledge is immutable. Do you, then, believe that God foreknows without willing or wills without knowing? If God foreknows as God wills, then God's will is eternal and unchanging (because God's nature is so), and if God wills as God foreknows, then divine knowledge is eternal and unchanging (because God's nature is so).[60]

From this it follows irrefutably that everything we do, everything that happens, even if it seems to us to happen mutably and contingently,[61] happens in fact nonetheless necessarily and immutably, if you have regard to the will of God. For the will of God is effectual and cannot be hindered, since it is the power of the divine nature itself; moreover it is wise, so that it cannot be deceived. Now, if God's will is not hindered, there is nothing to prevent the work itself from being done, in the place, time, manner, and measure that God both foresees and wills. If the will of God were such that, when the work was completed, the work remained but the will ceased—like the will of human beings, which ceases to will when the house they want is built, just as it also comes to an end in death—then it could be truly said that things happen contingently and mutably. But here the opposite happens; the work comes to an end and the will remains, so remote is it from possibility that the work itself, during its production and completed existence, should exist or persist contingently. To happen contingently, however—in order that we may not misuse terms—means in Latin, not that the work itself is contingent, but that it is done by a contingent and mutable will, such as there is not in God. Moreover, a work can only be called contingent when it happens contingently to us and in the way of chance without our expecting it, because our will or hand seizes on it as something presented to us by chance, when we have thought or willed nothing about it previously.

[I could wish indeed that another and a better word had been introduced into our discussion than this usual one, "necessity," which is not rightly applied either to the divine or the human will. It has too harsh and incongruous a meaning for this purpose, for it suggests a kind of compulsion, and the very opposite of willingness, although the subject under discussion implies no such thing. For neither the divine nor the human will does what it does, whether good or evil, under any compulsion, but from sheer pleasure or desire, as with true freedom;[62] and yet the will of God is immutable and infallible, and it governs our mutable will, as Boethius (c. 480–524)[63] sings: "Remaining fixed, You make all things move";[q] and our will, especially when it is evil, cannot of itself do good. The reader's intelligence must therefore supply what the word *necessity* does not express, by understanding it to mean what you might call the immutability of the will of God and the impotence of our evil will, or what some have called the necessity of immutability, though this is not very good either grammatically or theologically.][r]

The Sophists have labored for years over this point, but in the end they have been beaten and forced to admit that everything happens necessarily, though by the necessity of consequence (as

Scholastics used reason as a way to explain the compatibility of divine foreknowledge and human freedom. Later the "empiricist philosophers" with natural sciences, rejected the idea of chance or indeterminism, or an "uncaused cause," and looked for evidence of strict causality and determinism as necessary for responsible actions. The prevailing options for different positions in the matter are basically three: (1) Determinists (with varying degrees) hold that there is a strict causality at play in reality, and that there is only one possible future; (2) Compatibilists consider free will—itself caused—as compatible with determinism and human character being determined; (3) Libertarians deny the compatibility of free will with any determinism (incompatibilists).

**62.** This means, a will, agreeing to what is necessary, is not under compulsion but has some freedom, not in the sense of having a free choice between alternatives, but in the sense of being in compliance with God.

**63.** Boethius was a Roman philosopher and learned man who eventually served as an adviser to Ostrogoth king Theordoric (451/456–526). His enemies accused him of being disloyal to Theodoric and plotting to restore "Roman liberty." Theodoric imprisoned him and eventually had him executed. In some places he is honored as a Christian martyr, but it is not clear whether he was a Christian.

---

q   In Boethius, *De consolatione philosophiae* 3, 9.

r   This passage in brackets is an addition to Luther's text in the first edition of Luther's complete works.

**64.** This distinction means that some things have to follow necessarily others (the necessity of consequence), even if they are contingent in themselves (lacking the necessity of the consequent).

they say) and not by the necessity of the consequent.[64] They have thus eluded the full force of this question, or indeed it might rather be said they have deluded themselves. For how meaningless this is I shall have no difficulty in showing. What they call the necessity of consequence means broadly this: If God wills anything, it is necessary for that thing to come to pass, but it is not necessary that the thing which comes to pass should exist; for God alone exists necessarily, and it is possible for everything else not to exist if God so wills. So they say that an action of God is necessary if God wills it, but that the thing done is not itself necessary. But what do they achieve by this playing with words? This, of course, that the thing done is not necessary, in the sense that it has not a necessary existence. But this is no different from saying that the thing done is not of God. Nevertheless, it remains a fact that everything that comes into being does so necessarily, if the action of God is necessary, or if there is a necessity of consequence, however true it is that, when it has been brought into being, it does not exist necessarily, that is to say, it is not God and has not a necessary existence. For if I myself am brought into existence necessarily, it is of little concern to me that my being or becoming is mutable; for my contingent and mutable self, though not the necessary being that God is, is nonetheless brought into existence.

Hence their amusing idea, that everything happens by necessity of consequence but not by necessity of the consequent, amounts to no more than this: all things are indeed brought about necessarily, but when they have thus been brought about, they are not of God.[65] But what need was there to tell us this? As if there were any fear of our asserting that created things are God, or that they have a divine and necessary nature! Hence the proposition stands, and remains invincible, that all things happen by necessity. Nor is there here any obscurity or ambiguity. It says in Isaiah: "My counsel shall stand and my will shall be done" [Isa. 46:10]. What pupil does not know the meaning of these terms "counsel," "will," "shall be done," "shall stand"? [. . .]

**65.** What Luther summarizes here ironically means the distinction of the necessity of the consequence and of the consequent gave the Scholastics the possibility to state the full necessity of all actions, caused by God's immutable will, without making creatures necessary in themselves.

## [Should Divine Truth
## Be Kept from Common Ears?]

In the third chapter, you proceed to turn us into modest and peace-loving Epicureans, with a different sort of advice, though no sounder than the two already mentioned. That is to say, you tell us that some things are of such a kind that even if they were true and might be known, it would not be proper to divulge them before common ears.

Here again you confuse and mix everything up in your usual way, putting the sacred on a level with the profane and making no distinction between them at all, so that once again you have fallen into contempt and abuse of Scripture and of God. I said above that things that are either contained in or proved by the Holy Scriptures are not only plain, but also salutary, and can therefore safely be published, learned, and known, as indeed they ought to be. Hence your saying that they ought not to be divulged before common ears is false if you are speaking of the things that are in Scripture; and if you are speaking of other things, what you say does not interest us and is out of place, so that you are wasting your time and paper on it. Besides, you know that there is no subject on which I agree with the Sophists, so that you might well have spared me and not cast their misdoings in my teeth. For it was against me that you were to speak in that book of yours. I know where the Sophists go wrong without needing you to tell me, and they have had plenty of criticism from me. I should like this said once for all, and repeated every time you mix me up with the Sophists and make my case look as crazy as theirs, for you are being quite unfair, as you very well know.

Now, let us see the reasons for your advice. Even if it were true that "God, according to his own nature, is no less present in the hole of a beetle" or even in a sewer than in heaven (though you are too reverent to say this yourself, and blame the Sophists for blathering so), yet you think it would be unreasonable to discuss such a subject before the common herd.

First, let them blather who will; we are not here discussing what people do, but what is right and lawful, not how we live, but how we ought to live. Which of us always lives and acts rightly? But law and precept are not condemned on that account, but they rather condemn us.[66] Yet you go looking for irrelevancies like these, and rake a pile of them together from all sides, because this one point about the foreknowledge of God upsets you; and since you have no real argument with which to overcome it, you spend the time trying to tire out your reader with a lot of empty talk. But we will let that pass, and get back to the

66. This short remark relates to Luther's doctrine of the theological use of law that reveals sins.

subject. What, then, is the point of your contention that certain matters ought not to be discussed publicly? Do you count the subject of free choice among them? In that case, all I said above about the necessity of understanding free choice will round on you again. Moreover, why did you not follow your own advice and leave your *Diatribe* unwritten? If it is right for you to discuss free choice, why do you denounce such discussion? If it is wrong, why do you do it? On the other hand, if you do not count free choice among the prohibited subjects, you are again evading the real issue, dealing like a wordy rhetorician with topics that are irrelevant and out of place.

Even so, you are wrong in the use you make of this example, and in condemning as unprofitable the public discussion of the proposition that God is in the hole or the sewer. Your thoughts about God are all too human. There are, I admit, some shallow preachers who, from no motives of devotion or piety, but perhaps from a desire for popularity or a thirst for some novelty or a distaste for silence, prate and trifle in the shallowest way. But these please neither God nor people, even if they assert that God is in the heaven of heavens. But where there are serious and godly preachers who teach in modest, pure, and sound words, they speak on such a subject in public without risk, and indeed with great profit. Ought we not all to teach that the Son of God was in the womb of the Virgin and came forth from her belly? But how does a human belly differ from any other unclean place? Anyone could describe it in foul and shameless terms, but we rightly condemn those who do, seeing that there are plenty of pure words with which to speak of that necessary theme even with decency and grace. Again, the body of Christ himself was human as ours is, and what is fouler than that? Are we therefore not to say that God dwelt in it bodily, as Paul has said [Col. 2:9]?[67] What is fouler than death? What more horrifying than hell? Yet the prophet glories that God is present with him in death and hell [Ps. 139:8].

Therefore, a godly mind is not shocked to hear that God is present in death or hell, both of which are more horrible and foul than either a hole or a sewer. Indeed, since Scripture testifies that God is everywhere and fills all things [Jer. 23:24], a godly mind not only says that God is in those places, but must necessarily learn and know that God is there. Or are we to suppose that if I am captured by a tyrant and thrown into a prison or a

**67.** Luther is fighting here for a correct understanding of Christ's humanity; later on, in his struggle with Ulrich Zwingli (1484–1531), he had more opportunities to develop further his christological convictions, stressing the indivisible connection of both human and godly natures of Christ.

sewer—as has happened to many saints—I am not to be allowed to call upon God there or to believe that God is present with me, but must wait until I come into some finely furnished church?

If you teach us to talk such nonsense about God, and are so set against the locating of God's essence, you will end by not even allowing God to remain for us in heaven; for the heaven of heavens cannot contain God, nor is it worthy of God [1 Kings 8:27]. But as I have said, it is your habit to stab at us in this hateful way in order to disparage our case and make it odious, because you see that for you it is insuperable and invincible.

As for your second example, I admit that the idea that there are three Gods is a scandal if it is taught; but it is neither true, nor does Scripture teach it. The Sophists speak in this way with their newfound dialectic,[68] but what has that to do with us?[69] [...]

You, of course, always hold, or profess to hold, that human statutes can be observed without peril along with the Word of God. If they could, I should not hesitate to join you in the view you express here. So if you do not know it, I tell you again: human statutes cannot be observed together with the Word of God, because they bind consciences, while the Word sets them free. The two are as mutually incompatible as water and fire, unless the human statutes are kept freely, that is, as not being binding—a thing that the pope will not and cannot allow, unless he wants his kingdom ruined and brought to an end, since it is only maintained by the ensnaring and binding of consciences which the gospel asserts to be free. Therefore the authority of the Early Christian Teachers[s] is neither here nor there, and statutes wrongly enacted (as are all which are not in accordance with the Word of God) ought to be torn up and thrown away, for Christ ranks higher than the authority of these Teachers. In short, if this view of yours has reference to the Word of God, it is impious; if it refers to other things, your wordy argument in support of it is nothing to us, for we are arguing about the Word of God.

**68.** Dialectic was part of the seven liberal arts in medieval curriculum. It was mainly fulfilled by teaching of logic.

**69.** Roscelin of Compiègne (c. 1050–1125) in the eleventh century was accused of teaching about three godheads, but this seems to be a misunderstanding of his position.

s   Originally "Fathers."

## [Should the Truth
## of God's Necessitating Will Be Suppressed?]

In the last part of your Preface where you seriously try to dissuade me from my kind of doctrine, you think you have as good as won your point. What, you say, could be more useless than to publish this paradox to the world, that whatever is done by us is not done by free choice, but by sheer necessity? And Augustine's saying, that God works in us good and evil, and rewards God's own good works in us and punishes God's evil works in us[t]—what is the use of that? You are profuse in giving, or rather demanding, a reason here. What a window to impiety, you say, would the public avowal of this opinion open to finite human beings! What evildoer would correct his life? Who would believe he was loved by God? Who would war against one's own flesh? I am surprised that in your great vehemence and contentiousness you did not remember the point at issue and say: Where would free choice then remain?

My dear Erasmus, let me too say in turn: If you think these paradoxes are inventions of people, what are you contending about? Why are you so roused? Against whom are you speaking? Is there anyone in the world today who has more vigorously attacked the human dogmas than Luther? Therefore, your admonition has nothing to do with me. But if you think these paradoxes are words of God, how can you keep your countenance, where is your shame, where is—I will not say that well-known moderation of Erasmus, but the fear and reverence that are due to the true God, when you say that nothing more useless could be proclaimed than the Word of God? Naturally, your Creator must learn from you his creature what it is useful or useless to preach! That foolish, that thoughtless God did not previously know what ought to be taught until you, God's master, prescribed for God how to be wise and how to give commandments! As though God would not have known, if you had not been the teacher, that the consequences you mention would follow from this paradox! If, therefore, God has willed that such things should be openly spoken of and published abroad without regard to the consequences, who are you to forbid it?

---

t    Augustine, *De gratia Christi et de peccato originali* I, 17:18.

The apostle Paul, in his epistle to the Romans, discusses these same things, not in a corner, but publicly and before all the world, in the freest manner and in even harsher terms, when he says: "Whom he will he hardened," and, "God, willing to show God's wrath," etc. [Rom. 9:18, 22]. What could be harsher (to the unregenerate nature at least) than Christ's saying: "Many are called, but few chosen" [Matt. 22:14], or: "I know whom I have chosen" [John 13:18]? We have it, of course, on your authority that nothing more profitless could be said than things like these, because ungodly people are led by them to fall into desperation, hatred, and blasphemy.

Here, I see, you are of the opinion that the truth and usefulness of Scripture is to be measured and judged by the reactions of people, and the most ungodly people at that, so that only what has proved pleasing or seemed tolerable to them should be deemed true, divine, and salutary, while the opposite should forthwith be deemed useless, false, and pernicious. What are you aiming at with this advice, unless that the words of God should depend on, and stand or fall with, the choice and authority of human beings? Whereas Scripture says on the contrary that all things stand or fall by the choice and authority of God, and all the earth should keep silence before the Lord [Hab. 2:20]. To talk as you do, one must imagine the Living God to be nothing but a kind of shallow and ignorant ranter declaiming from some platform, whose words you can if you wish interpret in any direction you like, and accept or reject them accordingly as ungodly people are seen to be moved or affected by them. [. . .]

What then, you may ask, is the utility or necessity of publishing such things when so many evils appear to proceed from them? I answer: It would be enough to say that God has willed them to be published, and we must not ask the reason for the divine will, but simply adore it, giving God glory that, since God alone is just and wise, God does no wrong to anyone and can do nothing foolishly or rashly, though it may seem far otherwise to us. With this answer the godly are content. Still, out of our abundance we will do a work of supererogation and mention two considerations which demand that such things should be preached. The first is the humbling of our pride, and the knowledge of the grace of God; and the second is the nature of Christian faith itself.

**70.** This passage shows that it is not as easy to discern a theology of humility of Luther's younger years from his mature theology of justification, as some scholars (mainly Ernst Bizer) have suggested. See Ernst Bizer, *Fides ex auditu: eine Untersuchung über die Entdeckung der Gerechtigkeit Gottes durch Martin Luther* (Neukirchen: Verlag der Buchhandlung des Erziehungsvereins, 1958).

**71.** The concept of "desperation" in Luther's teaching is quite ambiguous: mostly he claims desperation to be the wrong way, while he stresses that human beings should respect their own inability (or disability) to "do the right" for salvation, without falling into desperation but instead finding the real ground for salvation in Jesus Christ.

First, God has assuredly promised grace to the humble [1 Peter 5:5], that is, to those who lament and despair of themselves.[70] But no human being can be thoroughly humbled until knowing that one's salvation is utterly beyond one's own powers, devices, endeavors, will, and works, and depends entirely on the choice, will, and work of another, namely, of God alone. For as long as one is persuaded that one can do even the least thing toward one's own salvation, the human being retains some self-confidence and does not altogether despair of oneself, and therefore is not humbled before God, but presumes that there is—or at least hopes or desires that there may be—some place, time, and work by which one may at length attain to salvation. But when one has no doubt that everything depends on the will of God, then one completely despairs[71] of oneself and chooses nothing for oneself, but waits for God to work; then this human being has come close to grace and can be saved.

It is thus for the sake of the elect that these things are published, in order that being humbled and brought back to nothingness by this means they may be saved. The rest resist this humiliation, indeed they condemn this teaching of self-despair, wishing for something, however little, to be left for them to do themselves; so they remain secretly proud and enemies of the grace of God. This, I say, is one reason, namely, that the godly, being humbled, may recognize, call upon, and receive the grace of God.

The second reason is that faith has to do with things not seen [Heb. 11:1]. Hence, in order that there may be room for faith, it is necessary that everything which is believed should be hidden. It cannot, however, be more deeply hidden than under an object, perception, or experience which is contrary to it. Thus, when God makes alive, God does it by killing; when God justifies, God does it by making human beings guilty; when God exalts to heaven by bringing down to hell, as Scripture says: "The LORD kills and brings to life; he brings down to Sheol and raises up" (1 Sam. 2[:6]). This is not the place to speak at length on this subject, but those who have read my books have had it quite plainly set forth for them.

Thus God hides divine eternal goodness and mercy under eternal wrath, God's righteousness under iniquity. This is the highest degree of faith, to believe God is merciful when saving so few and damning so many, and to believe God to be righteous when making us necessarily damnable, so that God seems, according to Erasmus, to delight in the torments of the wretched and to be worthy of hatred rather than of love. If, then, I could by any means comprehend how this God can be merciful and just who displays so much wrath and iniquity, there would be no need of faith. As it is, since that cannot be comprehended, there is room for the exercise of faith when such things are preached and published, just as when God kills, the faith of life is exercised in death. That is now enough by way of preface.

This way of dealing with people who argue about these paradoxes is better than yours. You advise silence and refusal to be drawn, with the idea of humoring their impiety; but you really achieve nothing by this. For if you either believe or suspect them to be true (since they are paradoxes of no small moment), such is the insatiable desire of mortals to probe into secret matters, especially when we most want them kept secret, that as a result of your publishing this warning everybody will now want to know all the more whether these paradoxes are true. They will have been aroused by your contention to such a degree that no one on our side will ever have provided such an opportunity for publicizing these paradoxes as you have done by this solemn and vehement warning. You would have been much wiser to say nothing at all about the need to beware of them if you wanted to see your desire fulfilled. The game is up when you do not directly deny that they are true; they cannot be kept dark, but the suspicion of their truth will prompt everybody to investigate them. Either, then, you must deny that they are true or set the example of silence if you want others to keep silence too.

## [Divine Necessity and the Human Will]

As for the second paradox, that whatever is done by us is done not by free choice but of sheer necessity, let us look briefly at this and not permit it to be labeled most pernicious. What I say here is this: When it has been proved that salvation is beyond our own powers and devices, and depends on the work of God alone (as I hope to prove conclusively below in the main body of this disputation), does it not follow that when God is not present in us by God's own means of work,[72] everything we do is evil, and we necessarily do what is of no avail for salvation? For if it is not we, but only God, who works salvation in us, then before God

72. Here Luther still shows his early mystical conviction of God being present in the believer.

works we can do nothing of saving significance, whether we wish to or not.

Now, by "necessarily" I do not mean "compulsorily," but by the necessity of immutability (as they say) and not of compulsion. That is to say, when human beings are without the Spirit of God, they do not do evil against their own will, as if they were taken by the scruff of the neck and forced to it, like a thief or robber carried off against their own will to punishment, but they do it of their own accord and with a ready will. And this readiness or will to act they cannot by their own powers omit, restrain, or change, but they keep on willing and being ready; and even if the human beings are compelled by external force to do something different, yet the will within them remains averse and they resent whatever compels or resists it. These human beings would not be resentful, however, if it were changed and they willingly submitted to the compulsion. This is what we call the necessity of immutability: It means that the will cannot change itself and turn in a different direction, but is rather the more provoked into willing by being resisted, as its resentment shows. This would not happen if it were free or had free choice. Ask experience how impossible it is to persuade people who have set their heart on anything. If they yield, they yield to force or to the greater attraction of something else; they never yield freely. On the other hand, if they are not set on anything, they simply let things take their course.

By contrast, if God works in us, the will is changed, and being gently breathed upon by the Spirit of God, it again wills and acts from pure willingness and inclination and of its own accord, not from compulsion, so that it cannot be turned another way by any opposition, nor be overcome or compelled even by the gates of hell, but it goes on willing and delighting in and loving the good, just as before it willed and delighted in and loved evil. This again is proved by experience, which shows how invincible and steadfast holy people are, who when force is used to compel them to other things are thereby all the more spurred on to will the good, just as fire is fanned into flames rather than extinguished by the wind. So not even here is there any free choice, or freedom to turn oneself in another direction or will something different, so long as the Spirit and grace of God remain in a human being.

In short, if we are under the god of this world, away from the work and Spirit of the true God, we are held captive to God's will, as Paul says to Timothy [2 Tim. 2:26], so that we cannot will anything but what God wills. For God is that strong man armed, who guards his own palace in such a way that those whom he possesses are in peace [Luke 11:21], so as to prevent them from stirring up any thought or feeling against him; otherwise, the kingdom of Satan being divided against itself would not stand [Luke 11:18], whereas Christ affirms that it does stand. And this we do readily and willingly, according to the nature of the will, which would not be a will if it were compelled; for compulsion is rather (so to say) "unwill." But if a Stronger One comes who overcomes him and takes us as One's spoil, then through this Spirit we are again slaves and captives—though this is royal freedom—so that we readily will and do what he wills. Thus the human will is placed between the two like a beast of burden. If God rides it, it wills and goes where God wills, as the psalm says: "I am become as a beast [before you] and I am always with you" [Ps. 73:22f.]. If Satan rides it, it wills and goes where Satan wills; nor can it choose to run to either of the two riders or to seek him out, but the riders themselves contend for the possession and control of it.[73]

What if I can prove from the words you yourself use in asserting freedom of choice that there is no free choice? What if I convict you of unwittingly denying what you seek so carefully to affirm? Frankly, unless I do so, I swear to regard everything I write against you in the entire book as revoked, and everything your *Diatribe* either asserts or queries against me as confirmed.

You make the power of free choice very slight and of a kind that is entirely ineffective apart from the grace of God. Do you not agree? Now I ask you, if the grace of God is absent or separated from it, what can that very slight power do of itself? It is ineffective, you say, and does nothing good. Then it cannot do what God or God's grace wills, at any rate if we suppose the grace of God to be separated from it. But what the grace of God does not do is not good. Hence it follows that free choice without the grace of God is not free at all, but immutably the captive and slave of evil, since it cannot of itself turn to the good. If this is granted, I give you leave to make the power of free choice, instead of something very slight, something angelic, indeed if possible something

**73.** "The simile of the beast and its riders was not Luther's own invention. He appears to have derived it from the pseudo-Augustinian *Hypomenesticon III.* xi.20, where it is connected, as Luther connects it, with Ps. 73.22f. . . . Yet Luther does not use it quite in the traditional way, for he equates the beast simply with the will (instead of free will) and makes the riders God and Satan (instead of sin and grace), and gives the beast no option as to which rider it shall have" (LW 33:66 n. 71).

quite divine; yet if you add this mournful rider, that apart from the grace of God it is ineffective, you at once rob it of all its power. What is ineffective power but simply no power at all?

Therefore, to say that free choice exists and has indeed some power, but that it is an ineffective power, is what the Sophists call *oppositum in adiecto* ["a contradiction in terms"]. It is as if you said that there is a free choice which is not free, which is as sensible as calling fire cold and earth hot. For fire may have the power of heat, even infernal heat, but if it does not burn or scorch, but is cold and freezes, let no one tell me it is a fire at all, much less a hot one, unless you mean a painted or imaginary fire. But if the power of free choice were said to mean that by which a human is capable of being taken hold of by the Spirit and imbued with the grace of God, as a being created for eternal life or death, no objection could be taken. For this power or aptitude, or as the Sophists say, this disposing quality or passive aptitude, we also admit; and who does not know that it is not found in trees or animals? For heaven, as the saying is, was not made for geese.[74]

It is settled, then, even on your own testimony, that we do everything by necessity, and nothing by free choice, since the power of free choice is nothing and neither does nor can do good in the absence of grace—unless you wish to give "efficacy" a new meaning and understand it as "perfection," as if free choice might very well make a start and will something, though it could not carry it through. But that I do not believe, and will say more about it later. It follows now that free choice is plainly a divine term, and can be properly applied to none but the Divine Majesty alone; for God alone can do and does (as the psalmist says [Ps. 115:3]) whatever pleases the divine will in heaven and on earth.[75] If this is attributed to human beings, it is no more rightly attributed than if divinity itself also were attributed to them, which would be the greatest possible sacrilege. Theologians therefore ought to have avoided this term when they wished to speak of human ability, leaving it to be applied to God alone. They should, moreover, have removed it from the lips and language of people, treating it as a kind of sacred and venerable name for their God. And if they attributed any power at all to men, they should teach that it must be called by another name than free choice, especially as we know and clearly perceive that the common people are miserably deceived and led astray by

**74.** Luther addresses Erasmus's definition of free choice in part 3 of this treatise and sums up the definition by quoting Erasmus: "By free choice in this place we mean a power of the human will by which a [person] can apply oneself to the things which lead to eternal salvation, or turn away from them" (see p. 198).

**75.** Luther here connects the question of the human will with the traditional definition of God's omnipotence, as stressed mainly in the late medieval *Via moderna*. The distinction of God's absolute and ordained power was one of the main topics to reflect on God's possibilities: while God's ordained power was bound to God's good will, God would not do all that God could do by means of the divine absolute power.

that term, since they hear and understand it in a very different sense from that which the theologians mean and discuss.

For the expression "free choice" is too imposing, too wide and full, and the people think it signifies—as the force and nature of the term requires—a power that can turn itself freely in either direction, without being under anyone's influence or control. If they knew that it was not so, but that hardly the tiniest spark of power was meant by this term, and a spark completely ineffectual by itself as a captive and slave of the devil, it would be surprising if they did not stone us as mockers and deceivers who say one thing and mean something quite different, or rather who have not yet decided or agreed on what we do mean. For one who speaks sophistically is hateful, as the Wise Person says [Prov. 6:17], particularly if one does this in matters of piety, where eternal salvation is at stake.

Since, then, we have lost the meaning and content of such a vainglorious term, or rather have never possessed it (as the Pelagians[76] wanted us to, who like you were led astray by the term), why do we so stubbornly hold on to an empty term, deceptive and dangerous as it is for the rank and file of believers? It is as sensible as when kings and princes hold on to or claim for themselves and boast about empty titles of kingdoms and countries, when in fact they are practically paupers and anything but the possessors of those kingdoms and countries. That, however, can be tolerated, since they deceive or mislead no one by it, but simply feed themselves on vanity, quite fruitlessly. But in the present case, there is a danger to salvation and a thoroughly injurious illusion.

Who would not think it ridiculous, or rather very objectionable, if some untimely innovator in the use of words attempted to introduce, against all common usage, such a manner of speaking as to call a beggar rich, not because he possessed any riches, but because some king might perhaps give him his, especially if this were done in seeming seriousness and not in a figure of speech, such as antiphrasis or irony. In this way, one who was mortally ill could be said to be perfectly well because some other might give him his own health, and a thoroughly illiterate fellow could be called very learned because someone else might perhaps give him learning. That is just how it sounds here: Human beings have free choice—if, of course, God would hand over them God's own will! By this misuse of language, anyone might boast

**76.** Pelagius (354–420) was the main counterpart of Augustine who was blamed to stress human beings' liberty concerning salvation. For Luther, medieval theology was, for the most part, "Pelagian" in this sense.

Portrait of reformer
John Wycliffe
(1324–1384)

of anything, as for instance, that human beings are the lords of heaven and earth—if God would grant it to them. But that is not the way for theologians to talk, but for stage players and public informers. Our words ought to be precise, pure, and sober, and as Paul says, sound and beyond censure [Titus 2:8].

But if we are unwilling to let this term go altogether—though that would be the safest and most God-fearing thing to do—let us at least teach human beings to use it honestly, so that free choice is allowed to them only with respect to what is beneath them and not what is above them. That is to say, human beings should know that with regard to their faculties and possessions they have the right to use, to do, or to leave undone, according to their own free choice, though even this is controlled by the free choice of God alone, who acts in whatever way God pleases. On the other hand, in relation to God, or in matters pertaining to salvation or damnation, a human being has no free choice, but is a captive, subject and slave either of the will of God or the will of Satan. [...]

# [Part II.
## Comments on Erasmus's Introduction]

### [The Evidence of Tradition
### on Behalf of Free Choice]

In introducing the Disputation, then, you promise to abide by the canonical Scriptures, since Luther holds himself bound by the authority of no other writer.[77] Very well, I accept your promise, although you do not give it because you regard those other writers as useless for your purpose, but in order to spare yourself fruitless labor. For you do not really approve of my audacity, or whatever else this principle of mine should be called. You are not a little impressed by such a numerous body of most learned men, who have found approval in so many centuries, among whom were some most skilled in divine studies, some of most godly life, some of them martyrs, many renowned for miracles, besides more recent theologians and so many universities, councils, bishops, and popes. In short, on that side stand erudition, genius, multitude, magnitude, altitude, fortitude, sanctity, miracles—

77. This means, at least for the purpose of the argument, that Erasmus accepted the *Sola scriptura* principle as the basis of the dispute, even if he did not adopt it in his theology.

A seventeenth-century
copper engraving
of Lorenzo Valla
(c. 1407–1457).

**78.** In fact, John Wycliffe (1324–1384) in his earlier writings had fully denied human free will due to predestination, while later on he admitted a limited freedom to human beings (*Responsiones ad Strodum*). Erasmus, in his *De libero arbitrio*, referred to the earlier, strong position of the English reformer, who was declared heretical by the Council of Constance, 1415.

**79.** Lorenzo (Laurentius) Valla (c. 1407–1457) was a humanist thinker, famous mainly for his proof that the emperor Constantine (c. 272–337) never gave his big "donation" of countries and power to the popes, as it was held for centuries. For Luther and Erasmus, he was interesting because of his treatise *De libero arbitrio*. Herein Valla denies the free will of human beings in an argument deriving from the notion of godly foreknowledge and tries to harmonize this position with the concept of a benevolent God. For Luther, it was important to have a humanist witness, such as Valla's, for the bound will. Erasmus counted Valla among the defenders of a bound will but added that he was not well reputed among theologians. Besides, he mentioned the Manicheans as opponents of the free will. This group, founded by Mani (242–277), held a completely dualistic view of the world and for this reason was attacked by Augustine and many others.

**80.** Erasmus meant to agree with Augustine of Hippo.

everything one could wish. On my side, however, there is only Wycliffe[78] and one other, Lorenzo Valla (c. 1407–1457)[79] (though Augustine, whom you overlook, is entirely with me[80]), and these carry no weight in comparison with those; so there remains only Luther, a private individual and a mere upstart, with his friends, among whom there is no such erudition or genius, no multitude or magnitude, no sanctity, no miracles—for they could not even cure a lame horse. They make a parade of Scripture, yet they are as uncertain about it as the other side, and though they boast of the Spirit, they give no sign of possessing it; and there are other things "which at great length you could recount." So it is the same with us as the wolf said to the nightingale he had devoured, "You are a voice and nothing more." They talk, you say, and for this alone they want to be believed.

I confess, my dear Erasmus, that you have good reason to be moved by all these things. I myself was so impressed by them for

**81.** In his lecture on the *Sentences*, Luther, indeed, maintained the liberty of human will. He seems to think of his *Heidelberg Disputation* (1518) as the public expression of his critical position against it. Historically, one can describe a long development of this position with important steps taken in his lectures on the Romans (1515–1516).

**82.** The following is an example of Luther's approach to the theologians of the early church. Luther respected them seriously, but he was also convinced that their words had to be measured by the Holy Scripture.

more than ten years[81] that I think no one else has ever been so disturbed by them. I, too, found it incredible that this Troy of ours, which for so long a time and through so many wars had proved invincible, could ever be taken. And I call God to witness on my soul, I should have continued so, I should be just as moved today, but for the pressure of my conscience and the evidence of facts that compel me to a different view. You can well imagine that my heart is not of stone; and even if it were, it could well have melted in the great waves and storms with which it had to struggle and the buffeting it received when I dared to do what I saw would bring down all the authority of those whom you have listed like a flood upon my head.

But this is not the place to tell the story of my life or works, nor have we undertaken these things in order to commend ourselves, but in order to extol the grace of God. The sort of person I am, and the spirit and purpose with which I have been drawn into this affair, I leave to God, who knows that all these things have been effected by his free choice, not mine—though the whole world itself ought to have been long ago aware of this. You clearly put me into a very unpleasant position by this Introduction of yours, since I cannot easily get out of it without singing my own praises and censuring so many of the Teachers of the Early Church.[82] But I will be brief. In erudition, genius, the number of authorities supporting me, and everything else I am, as you rightly judge, inferior. But suppose I ask you what *is* a manifestation of the Spirit, what miracles are, what sanctity is; to these three questions, so far as I know you from your letters and books, you would seem to be too inexperienced and ignorant to give one syllable of an answer. Or if I should press you to say which human being, of all those you boast about, you can certainly show to have been or to be a saint, or to have had the Spirit, or to have performed real miracles, I think you would have to work very hard at it, and all to no purpose. You repeat many things that are commonly said and publicly preached, and you do not realize how much credibility and authority they lose when summoned to the bar of conscience. It is a true proverb that many pass for saints on earth whose souls are in hell.

But we will grant you, if you wish, that they all were saints, all had the Spirit, all performed miracles—though you do not ask for this. Tell me this: Was it in the name or by the power of free choice, or to confirm the dogma of free choice, that any of them became a saint, received the Spirit, and performed miracles? Far from it, you will say; it was in the name and by the power of Jesus Christ, and in support of the doctrine of Christ, that all these things were done. Why, then, do you adduce their sanctity, their possession of the Spirit, and their miracles in support of the dogma of free choice when these were not given or done for that purpose? Their miracles, their possession of the Spirit, and their sanctity, therefore, speak for us who preach Jesus Christ and not the powers or works of people. Now, how is it surprising if those individuals, holy, spiritual, and workers of miracles as they were, sometimes under the influence of the flesh spoke and acted according to the flesh, when this happened more than once even to the apostles in the time of Christ himself? For you yourself do not deny, but assert, that free choice is not a matter of the Spirit or of Christ, but a human affair, so that the Spirit, who was promised in order to glorify Christ [John 16:14] could in any case not preach free choice. If, therefore, the Teachers of the Early Church[u] have sometimes preached free choice, they have certainly spoken from carnal motives (since they were but human beings) and not by the Spirit of God, and much less have they performed miracles in support of free choice. So what you say about the sanctity, Spirit, and miracles of the Fathers is beside the point, since what is proved by them is not free choice but the dogma of Jesus Christ as opposed to the dogma of free choice. [. . .]

And what I have said about miracles, I say also about sanctity. If from such a series of ages, people, and everything else you have mentioned, you can show one work (if only the lifting of a straw from the ground), or one word (if only the syllable "my"), or one thought (if only the faintest sigh), arising from the power of free choice, by which they have applied themselves to grace or merited the Spirit or obtained pardon or done anything alongside God, however slight (I do not say by which they have been sanctified), then again you shall be the victors and we the vanquished—by the power, I say, and in the name of free choice. (For the things that are done in human beings by the power of divine creation have testimonies of Scripture in abundance.) And you certainly ought to give such a demonstration, unless you want

*u*   See n. 82, p. 186.

**83.** "The Stoics, from Zeno the founder of the school (at Athens, c. 308 BCE) to Seneca, Epictetus, and Marcus Aurelius, portrayed as ideal a [hu]man for whom virtue was the highest good, who was in strict control of one's passions, indifferent to pleasure or pain, and unmoved by such things as family affection, or any kind of calamity or misfortune" (LW 33:76 n. 8).

to look ridiculous as teachers by spreading dogmas through the world with such a superior air and such authority about a thing for which you produce no tangible evidence. Otherwise, they will be called dreams and of no consequence whatever, which is by far the most shameful thing that could happen to such great people of so many centuries with all their learning and sanctity and their power to work miracles. In that case we shall prefer the Stoics[83] to you, for although even they pictured such a wise individual as they never saw, yet they did endeavor to express some aspect of him in their lives. You people are not able to express anything at all, not even the shadow of your dogma.

I say the same with regard to the Spirit. If out of all the assertors of free choice you can show a single one who has had the strength of mind or feeling even in such small degree as to be able in the name and by the power of free choice to look beyond a single farthing, to forgo a single crumb, or to bear a single word or gesture of ill will (to say nothing of despising wealth, life, and reputation), then take the palm again, and we will willingly admit defeat. And this you really ought to demonstrate to us, after all your bragging words about the power of free choice, or again you will seem to be wrangling about goat's wool, like the man who watched the play in an empty theater. But I can easily show you, on the contrary, that holy people such as you boast about, whenever they come to pray or plead with God, approach God in utter forgetfulness of their own free choice, despairing of themselves and imploring nothing but pure grace alone, though they have merited something very different. This was often the case with Augustine, and it was so with Bernard when, at the point of death, he said, "I have lost my time, because I have lived like a lost soul."[v] I do not see that any power is claimed here which could apply itself to grace, but every power is accused of having done nothing but turn away from grace. It is true that these same saints sometimes in their disputations spoke differently about free choice, but that is just what I see happening to everybody; they are different when they are intent on words or arguments from what they are when they are concerned with feelings and actions. In the former case, they speak differently from what they previously felt, and in the latter, they feel differ-

---

v    Bernard of Clairvaux (1090–1153), *Sermo in Canticum Canticorum* 20,1. This sentence was quoted very often by Luther.

ently from what they previously said. But human beings are to be measured by their affections rather than their talk, whether they are godly or ungodly.

But we grant you still more. We do not demand miracles, the Spirit, sanctity; we return to the dogma itself. All we ask is that you should at least indicate to us what work or word or thought this power of free choice stirs up, attempts, or performs, in order to apply itself to grace. It is not enough to say, "There is a power, there is a power, there is a definite power of free choice," for what is easier to say than this? Nor is this worthy of those most learned and holy people who have found approval in so many centuries. The child must be named, as the German proverb says. We must have a definition of what that power is, what it does, what it suffers, what happens to it. For example, to put it very crudely, the question is whether this power has a duty, or makes an attempt, to pray, or fast, or labor, or discipline the body, or give alms, or anything else of this kind; for if it is a power, it must do some sort of work. But here you are dumber than Seriphian frogs and fishes.[84] And how could you give a definition, when on your own testimony you are still uncertain about the power itself, disagreeing with each other and inconsistent with yourselves? What is to be done about a definition when the thing defined does not itself remain constant? [. . .]

### [The True Church, Which Does Not Err, Is Hidden from Human Sight]

This is my answer to your statement that it is incredible that God should have concealed an error in his Church for so many centuries, and should not have revealed to any of his saints what we claim to be the chief doctrine of the gospel. First, we do not say that this error has been tolerated by God in God's Church or in any of God's saints. For the Church is ruled by the Spirit of God and the saints are led by the Spirit of God (Rom. 8[:14]). And Christ remains with his Church even to the end of the world [Matt. 28:20]; and the Church of God is the pillar and ground of the truth [1 Tim. 3:15]. These things, I say, we know; for the creed that we all hold affirms, "I believe in the holy catholic church"; so that it is impossible for the Church to err, even in the smallest article. And even if we grant that some of the elect are bound in error all their lives, yet they must necessarily return to the right

84. The Seriphian frogs means dumb persons; cf. Erasmus, *Adagia* 1,5,31.

**85.** The arguments Luther adopts here were used in late medieval ecclesiological debates, where authors showed that God's promises to the church that it would not err did not necessarily refer to ecclesiastical institutions but to the crowd of believers.

**86.** "The followers of Arius (c. 250–336), presbyter of Alexandria, were excommunicated in 318 for denying the divinity of Christ. His teaching, variously modified, won widespread acceptance and had the support of several emperors before the orthodox doctrine, formulated at the Council of Nicaea in 325, finally prevailed" (LW 33:86 n. 30).

way before they die, since Christ says in John 10[:28]: "No one shall snatch them out of my hand."

But here is the task, here is the toil, to determine whether those whom you call the Church are the Church, or rather, whether after being in error all their lives they were at last brought back before they died. For it does not immediately follow that if God has permitted all those whom you quote, from as many centuries as you like and most learned though they were, to be in error, therefore God has permitted his Church to err.[85] Look at Israel, the people of God, where in so long a line of kings over so long a period of time not a single king is listed who did not err. And in the time of the prophet Elijah, everybody and everything in the public life of this people had so far fallen into idolatry that Elijah thought he alone was left [1 Kings 18:22]; and yet, although kings, princes, priests, prophets, and everything that could be called the People or Church of God was going to perdition, God had kept seven thousand [1 Kings 19:18]. But who saw them, or knew them to be the People of God? Who, then, even at the present time would venture to deny that, concealed under those outstanding figures—for you mention none but persons of public office and distinction—God has preserved for Godself a Church among the common people, and has permitted those others to perish as God did in the kingdom of Israel? For it is characteristic of God to lay low the picked people of Israel and slay their strong ones (Ps. 78[:31]), but to preserve the dregs and remnant of Israel, as Isaiah says [10:22].

What happened in Christ's own time, when all the apostles fell away [Matt. 26:31, 56] and he himself was denied and condemned by the whole people, and scarcely more than a Nicodemus, a Joseph, and the thief on the cross were saved? Were these then called the People of God? They were the remnant of the People, but they were not so called, and what was so called was not the People of God. Who knows but that the state of the Church of God throughout the whole course of the world from the beginning has always been such that some have been called the People and the saints of God who were not so, while others, a remnant in their midst, really were the People or the saints, but were never called so, as witness the stories of Cain and Abel, Ishmael and Isaac, Esau and Jacob? Look at the time of the Arians,[86] when scarcely five Catholic bishops were preserved in the whole world, and they were driven from their sees, while the Arians reigned everywhere in the public name and office of the Church; nevertheless, Christ preserved his Church under these heretics, though in such a way that it was far from being recognized and regarded as the Church.

Under the reign of the pope, show me one bishop discharging his duty, show me one Council that has been concerned with matters of piety rather than robes, rank, revenues, and other profane trifles, which no one who was not insane could attribute to the Holy Spirit. Yet they are nonetheless called the Church, although all of them, at least while they live like this, are reprobates and anything but the Church. Yet even under them Christ has preserved his Church, but not so as to have it called the Church. How many saints do you suppose the minions of the Inquisition alone have burned and murdered during the last few centuries? I mean persons like John Hus, in whose time without doubt there lived many holy people in the same spirit.[87] [. . .]

87. Jan Hus (c. 1369–1415), preacher for a pure church in Bohemia, was burned as a heretic at the Council of Constance in 1415.

But to return to the point. How is it surprising if God allows all the great ones of the Church to walk in their own ways, when God has thus allowed all the nations to walk in their own ways, as Paul says in Acts [14:16]? The Church of God is not as commonplace a thing, my dear Erasmus, as the phrase "the Church of God"; nor are the saints of God met with as universally as the phrase "the saints of God." They are a pearl and precious jewels, which the Spirit does not cast before swine [Matt. 7:6] but keeps hidden, as Scripture says [Matt. 11:25], lest the ungodly should see the glory of God. Otherwise, if they were plainly recognized by all, how could they possibly be as harassed and afflicted in the world as they are? As Paul says: "If they had known, they would not have crucified the Lord of glory" [1 Cor. 2:8]. [. . .]

## [Scripture, with Its "Internal" and "External" Clarity, as the Test of Truth]

What, then, are we to do? The Church is hidden,[88] the saints are unknown. What and whom are we to believe? Or, as you very pointedly argue, who gives us certainty? How shall we prove the Spirit? If you look for learning, on both sides there are scholars; if for quality of life, on both sides are sinners; if for Scripture, both sides acknowledge it. But the dispute is not so much about Scripture which may not yet be sufficiently clear, as about

88. This is a central conviction of Luther's ecclesiology, that only God sees the true members of the church.

the meaning of Scripture; and on both sides are men, of whom neither numbers nor learning nor dignity, much less fewness, ignorance, and humility, have anything to do with the case. The matter therefore remains in doubt and the case is still *sub judice*,ᵂ so that it looks as if we might be wise to adopt the position of the Skeptics, unless the line you take is best, when you express your uncertainty in such a way as to aver that you are seeking to learn the truth, though in the meantime you incline to the side that asserts free choice, until the truth becomes clear. [ . . . ]

What we say is this: The spirits are to be tested or proved by two sorts of judgment. One is internal, whereby through the Holy Spirit or a special gift of God, anyone who is enlightened concerning himself and his own salvation, judges and discerns with the greatest certainty the dogmas and opinions of all people. Of this it is said in 1 Cor. 1 [2:15]: "The spiritual person judges all things but is judged by no one." This belongs to faith and is necessary for every individual Christian. We have called it above "the internal clarity of Holy Scripture." Perhaps this was what those had in mind who gave you the reply that everything must be decided by the judgment of the Spirit. But this judgment helps no one else, and with it we are not here concerned, for no one, I think, doubts its reality.

There is therefore another, an external judgment, whereby with the greatest certainty we judge the spirits and dogmas of all men, not only for ourselves, but also for others and for their salvation. This judgment belongs to the public ministry of the Word and to the outward office, and is chiefly the concern of leaders and preachers of the Word. We make use of it when we seek to strengthen those who are weak in faith and confute opponents. This is what we earlier called "the external clarity of Holy Scripture."⁸⁹ Thus we say that all spirits are to be tested in the presence of the Church at the bar of Scripture. For it ought above all to be settled and established among Christians that the Holy Scriptures are a spiritual light far brighter than the sun itself, especially in things that are necessary to salvation. But because we have for so long been persuaded of the opposite by that pestilential saying of the Sophists that the Scriptures are obscure and ambiguous, we are obliged to begin by proving

**89.** For Luther the "clarity of Holy Scripture" meant that through the Bible, God's word is clear and accessible to those who hear it. Matters of doctrine and faith are made clear in Scripture, which then becomes the primary guide, especially in things necessary for salvation. This is in contrast to the church's teaching that Scripture is unclear without the explanation offered by the scholars or officials of the church. In Luther's contrasting view, because of Scripture's clarity, people do not need to to have it explained or interpreted by a pope or council in order for its meaning to be understood.

*w*   Latin for "under judgment."

even that first principle of ours by which everything else has to be proved—a procedure that among the philosophers would be regarded as absurd and impossible.[90] [. . .]

But here you will say, "All this is nothing to me; I do not say that the Scriptures are obscure in all parts (for who would be so crazy?), but only in this and similar parts." I reply: neither do I say these things in opposition to you only, but in opposition to all who think as you do;[91] moreover, in opposition to you I say with respect to the whole Scripture, I will not have any part of it called obscure. What we have cited from Peter holds well here, that the Word of God is for us "a lamp shining in a dark place" [2 Pet. 1:19]. But if part of this lamp does not shine, it will be a part of the dark place rather than of the lamp itself. Christ has not so enlightened us as deliberately to leave some part of his Word obscure while commanding us to give heed to it, for he commands us in vain to give heed if it does not give light.

Consequently, if the dogma of free choice is obscure or ambiguous, it does not belong to Christians or the Scriptures, and it should be abandoned and reckoned among those fables that Paul condemns Christians for wrangling about. If, however, it does belong to Christians and the Scriptures, it ought to be clear, open, and evident, exactly like all the other clear and evident articles of faith. For all the articles of faith held by Christians ought to be such that they are not only most certain to Christians themselves, but also fortified against the attacks of others by such manifest and clear Scriptures that they shut all men's mouths and prevent their saying anything against them; as Christ says in his promise to us: "I will give you a mouth and wisdom, which none of your adversaries will be able to withstand" [Luke 21:15]. If, therefore, our mouth is so weak at this point that our adversaries can withstand it, his saying that no adversary can withstand our mouth is false. Either, therefore, we shall have no adversaries while maintaining the dogma of free choice (which will be the case if free choice does not belong to us), or if it does belong to us, we shall have adversaries, it is true, but they will not be able to withstand us.

But this inability of the adversaries to withstand (since the point arises here) does not mean that they are compelled to abandon their own position, or are persuaded either to confess or keep silence. For who can compel people against their will

**90.** Luther thinks of the denial of circling arguments.

**91.** A remark like this shows Luther's awareness of the public debate among the learned readers potentially in all Europe.

to believe, to confess their error, or to be silent? "What is more loquacious than vanity?" as Augustine says.[x] But what is meant is that their mouth is so far stopped that they have nothing to say in reply and, although they say a great deal, yet in the judgment of common sense they say nothing. This is best shown by examples.

When Christ in Matthew 22[:23ff.] put the Sadducees to silence by quoting Scripture and proving the resurrection of the dead from the words of Moses in Exodus 3[:6]: "I am the God of Abraham," etc.; "This is not the God of the dead, but of the living," here they could not resist or say anything in reply. But did they therefore give up their own opinion? And how often did he confute the Pharisees by the plainest Scriptures and arguments, so that the people clearly saw them convicted, and even they themselves perceived it? Nevertheless, they continued to be his adversaries. Stephen in Acts 7 [6:10] spoke, according to Luke, in such a way that they could not withstand the wisdom and the Spirit with which he spoke. But what did they do? Did they give way? On the contrary, being ashamed to be beaten, and not being able to withstand, they went mad, and shutting their ears and eyes they set up false witnesses against him (Acts 8 [6:11–14]).

See how this man stands before the Council and confutes his adversaries! After enumerating the benefits which God had bestowed on that people from the beginning, and proving that God had never ordered a temple to be built for God (for this was the question at issue and the substance of the charge against him), he at length concedes that a temple was in fact built under Solomon, but then he qualifies it in this way: "Yet the Most High does not dwell in houses made with hands," and in proof of this he quotes Isaiah 66[:1]: "What house is this that you build for me?" Tell me, what could they say here against so plain a Scripture? Yet they were quite unmoved and remained set in their own opinion; which leads him to attack them directly, in the words: "Uncircumcised in heart and ears, you always withstand the Holy Spirit," etc. [Acts 7:51]. He says they withstand, although they were unable to withstand.

Let us come to our own times. When Jan Hus[y] argues as follows against the pope on the basis of Matthew 16[:18]: "The gates

---

x    Augustine, *De civitate Dei* 5:26.

y    Jan Hus, *De ecclesia*, ch. 7.

of hell do not prevail against my church" (is there any ambiguity or obscurity here?), "but against the pope and his followers the gates of hell do prevail, for they are notorious the world over for their open impiety and wickedness" (is this also obscure?), "therefore the pope and his followers are not the church of which Christ speaks"—what could they say in reply to this, or how could they withstand the mouth that Christ had given him? Yet they did withstand, and they persisted until they burned him, so far were they from altering their opinion. Nor does Christ overlook this when he says, "Your adversaries will not be able to withstand." They are adversaries, he says; therefore, they will withstand, for otherwise they would not be adversaries but friends; and yet they will not be able to withstand. What else does this mean but that in withstanding they will not be able to withstand?

If, accordingly, we are able so to confute free choice that our adversaries cannot withstand, even if they persist in their own opinion and withstand in spite of their conscience, we shall have done enough. For I have had enough experience to know that no one wants to be beaten and, as Quintilian says, there is no one who would not rather seem to know than to learn,[z] though it is a sort of proverb on everyone's lips nowadays (from use, or rather abuse, more than from conviction): "I wish to learn, I'm ready to be taught, and when shown a better way, to follow it; I'm only human, and I may be wrong." The fact is that under this mask, this fair show of humility, they find it possible quite confidently to say: "I'm not satisfied, I don't see it, he does violence to the Scriptures, he's an obstinate assertor"; because, of course, they are sure that no one will suspect such very humble souls of stubbornly resisting and even vigorously attacking recognized truth. So it is made to seem that their refusal to alter their opinion ought not to be set down to their own perverseness, but to the obscurity and ambiguity of the arguments. [...]

## [Erasmus Is in a Dilemma]

Why do I go on? Why do we not end the case with this Introduction, and pronounce sentence on you from your own words, according to that saying of Christ: "By your words you will be justified, and by your words you will be condemned" [Matt. 12:37]?

---

z    Quintilian, *Institutiones* 3:1,6.

**92.** A diatribe means "collation" or "discourse"; an *apophasis* refers to the raising of an issue by claiming not to mention it, or introducing a topic while denying that it should be brought up (e.g., "I will by no means speak of my opponent's faulty reasoning").

For you say that Scripture is not crystal clear on this point, and then you suspend judgment and discuss both sides of the question, asking what can be said for it and what against; and you do nothing else in the whole of this book, which for that reason you have chosen to call a diatribe rather than an apophasis[92] or anything else, because you write with the intention of collating everything and affirming nothing.

If, then, Scripture is not crystal clear, how is it that those of whom you boast are not only blind at this point, but rash and foolish enough to define and assert free choice on the basis of Scripture, as though it were quite positive and plain? I mean your numerous body of most learned individuals who have found approval in so many centuries down to our day, most of whom have godliness of life as well as a wonderful skill in divine studies to commend them, and some gave testimony with their blood to the doctrine of Christ that they had defended with their writings. If you say this sincerely, it is a settled point with you that free choice has assertors endowed with a wonderful skill in the Holy Scriptures, and that such individuals even bore witness to it with their blood. If that is true, they must have regarded Scripture as crystal clear; otherwise, what meaning would there be in that wonderful skill they had in the Holy Scriptures? Besides, what levity and temerity of mind it would argue to shed their blood for something uncertain and obscure! That is not the act of martyrs of Christ, but of demons!

Now, you also should "consider whether more weight ought not to be ascribed to the previous judgments of so many learned authors, so many orthodox, so many saints, so many martyrs, so many theologians old and new, so many universities, councils, bishops, and popes," who have found the Scriptures crystal clear and have confirmed this both by their writings and their blood, or to your own "private judgment" alone when you deny that the Scriptures are crystal clear, and when perhaps you have never shed a single tear or uttered one sigh on behalf of the doctrine of Christ. If you think those individuals were right, why do you not imitate them? If you do not think so, why do you rant and brag with such a spate of words, as if you wanted to overwhelm me with a sort of tempest and deluge of oratory—which nevertheless falls with the greater force on your own head, while my ark rides aloft in safety? For you attribute to all these great individuals the greatest folly and temerity when you describe them as so highly skilled in Scripture and as having asserted it by their pen, their life and their death, although you maintain that it is obscure and ambiguous. This is nothing else but to make them most inexpert in knowledge and most foolish in assertion. I should not have paid them such a compliment in my private contempt of them as you do in your public commendation of them.

I have you here, therefore, on the horns of a dilemma,[93] as they say. For one or the other of these two things must be false; either your saying that those individuals were admirable for their skill in the Holy Scriptures, their life, and their martyrdom or your saying that Scripture is not crystal clear. But since you are drawn rather to believing that the Scriptures are not crystal clear (for that is what you are driving at throughout your book), we can only conclude that you have described those individuals as experts in Scripture and martyrs for Christ either in fun or in flattery and in no way seriously, merely in order to throw dust into the eyes of the uneducated public and make difficulties for Luther by loading his cause with odium and contempt by means of empty words. I, however, say that neither statement is true, but both are false. I hold, first, that the Scriptures are entirely clear; secondly, that those individuals, insofar as they assert free choice, are most inexpert in the Holy Scriptures; and thirdly, that they made this assertion neither by their life nor their death, but only with their pen—and that while their wits were wandering.

I therefore conclude this little debate as follows. By means of Scripture, regarded as obscure, nothing definite has ever yet been settled or can be settled concerning free choice, on your own testimony. Moreover, by the lives of all human beings from the beginning of the world, nothing has been demonstrated in favor of free choice, as has been said above. Therefore, to teach something which is neither prescribed by a single word inside the Scriptures nor demonstrated by a single fact outside them is no part of Christian doctrine, but belongs to the *True History* of Lucian,[94] except that Lucian, by making sport with ludicrous subjects in deliberate jest, neither deceives nor harms anyone, whereas these friends of ours with their insane treatment of a serious subject, and one that concerns eternal salvation, lead innumerable souls to perdition.

In this way I also might have put an end to this whole question about free choice, seeing that even the testimony of my

**93.** In the Latin text, Luther here speaks of a syllogism. This means the most important logical technique, concluding one sentence from two others, e.g.: Socrates is a human being. All human beings are mortal. Thus, Socrates is mortal.

**94.** Lucian's *Vera historiae* was a parody about Homer and others.

adversaries favors my position and conflicts with theirs, and there can be no stronger proof than the personal confession and testimony of a defendant against oneself. But since Paul bids us silence empty talkers [Titus 1:10f.], let us go into the details of the case and deal with the subject in the order in which the *Diatribe* proceeds, first confuting the arguments adduced in favor of free choice, then defending arguments of our own that have been attacked, and lastly contending against free choice on behalf of the grace of God.

# [Part III. Refutation of Arguments in Support of Free Choice]

### [Erasmus's Definition of Free Choice]

Now first we will begin quite properly with the definition you give of free choice, where you say: "By free choice in this place we mean a power of the human will by which one can apply oneself to the things which lead to eternal salvation, or turn away from them." It is very prudent of you to give only a bare definition and not to explain (as others usually do) any part of it—perhaps because you were afraid you might be shipwrecked on more than one point. I am thus compelled to look at your definition in detail. What is defined, certainly if it is examined closely, is wider than the definition, which is of a kind that the Sophists would call "vicious," a term they apply whenever a definition does not exhaust the thing defined. For we have shown above that free choice properly belongs to no one but God alone. You might perhaps rightly attribute some measure of choice to human beings, but to attribute free choice to them in relation to divine things is too much; for the term "free choice," in the judgment of everyone's ears, means (strictly speaking) that which can do and does, in relation to God, whatever it pleases, uninhibited by any law or any sovereign authority. For you would not call a slave free, who acts under the sovereign authority of one's master; and still less rightly can we call a human being or angel free, when they live under the absolute sovereignty of God (not to mention sin and death) in such a way that they cannot subsist for a moment by their own strength.

Here, therefore, at the very outset, there is a conflict between the nominal definition of the real definition,[95] because the term signifies one thing and the real item is understood as another.[96] It would be more correct to speak of "vertible choice" or "mutable choice,"[97] in the way in which Augustine and the Sophists after him limit the glory and range of the word *free* by introducing the disparaging notion of what they call the vertibility of free choice. In such a way it would be fitting for us to speak, to avoid deceiving the hearts of human beings with inflated and high-sounding but empty words; just as Augustine also thinks we ought to make it a definite rule to speak only in sober and strictly appropriate words. For in teaching, simplicity and appropriateness of speech is required, not bombast and persuasive rhetorical images.[98] But in order not to appear to delight in quarreling about words, let us for the moment accept this misuse of terms, serious and dangerous though it is, and allow free choice to be the same as vertible choice. Let us also grant Erasmus his point when he makes free choice a power of the human will, as if angels did not have free choice, since in his book he has undertaken to deal only with the free choice of human beings; otherwise, in this respect too the definition would be narrower than the thing defined.

Let us come to those parts of the definition on which the whole matter hinges. Some of them are plain enough, but others shun the light as though guiltily aware that they have everything to fear; yet nothing ought to be more plainly and unhesitatingly expressed than a definition, since to define obscurely is the same as giving no definition at all. The plain parts are these: "a power of the human will," "by which a human being is able," and "to eternal salvation"; but the following are like blindfolded gladiators: "to apply," "to the things which lead," and "to turn away." How are we going to divine what this applying and turning away means? And what are the "things which lead to eternal salvation"? What is all this about? I am dealing, I see, with a real Scotus[99] or Heraclitus,[100] and am to be worn out by the double labor involved. For first I have to go groping nervously about amid pitfalls and darkness (which is a venturesome and risky thing to do) in quest of my adversary, and unless I find him I shall be tilting at ghosts and beating the air in the dark. Then if I do manage to drag him into the light, I shall have to come to grips with him on equal terms when I am already wearied with looking for him.

95. Luther here shows his good scholastic education: nominal definition and real definition were two different types of definition in late medieval logic, the first concerning the logical impact of the definition, the second including the reference to the real world outside the human mind.

96. The theory of signification also was one of the most discussed matters in late medieval philosophy. According to it, one's understanding of terms depends from the right signifying relation to the items meant by them.

97. E.g., Thomas of Aquinas, *Summa theologiae* II-II q. 24 a. 11 respondeo.

98. This is a clear adaption of the rules of late medieval *Via moderna* to avoid a plurality of words. One has to reduce the number of words, using just some words with clear signification.

99. Duns Scotus, the so called *Doctor subtilis*, was known for his intricate scholastic arguments.

100. Heraclitus, a Pre-Socratic philosopher well known for his sentence: "Everything flows." His work was regarded as quite obscure.

I take it, then, that what is meant by "a power of the human will" is a capacity or faculty or ability or aptitude for willing, unwilling, selecting, neglecting, approving, rejecting, and whatever other actions of the will there are. Now, what it means for that same power to "apply itself" and to "turn away" I do not see, unless it is precisely this willing and unwilling, selecting, neglecting, approving, rejecting, or in other words, precisely the action of the will. So that we must imagine this power to be something between the will itself and its action, as the means by which the will itself produces the action of willing and unwilling, and by which the action of willing and unwilling is itself produced. Anything else it is impossible either to imagine or conceive here. If I am mistaken, let the author be blamed who has given the definition, not I who am trying to understand it; for as the lawyers rightly say, if one speaks obscurely when one could speak more clearly, one's words are to be interpreted against oneself. And here for the moment I want to forget my Modernist friends[101] with their subtleties, since there is need of plain, blunt speaking for the sake of teaching and understanding.

Now, the things which lead to eternal salvation I take to be the words and works of God that are presented to the human will so that it may apply itself to them or turn away from them. By the words of God, moreover, I mean both the law and the gospel, the law requiring works and the gospel faith.[102] For there is nothing else that leads either to the grace of God or to eternal salvation except the word and work of God, since grace or the Spirit is life itself, to which we are led by God's word and work. [. . .]

On the authority of Erasmus, then, free choice is a power of the will that is able of itself to will and unwill (*nolle*)[a] the word and work of God, by which it is led to those things which exceed both its grasp and its perception. But if it can will and unwill, it can also love and hate, and if it can love and hate, it can also in some small degree do the works of the law and believe the gospel. For if you can will or unwill anything, you must to some extent be able to perform something by that will, even if someone else prevents your completing it. Now, in that case, since the works of God that lead to salvation include death, the cross, and all the

**101.** The "modernists" shaped the so-called *Via moderna* in the late Middle Ages as an alternative to the *Via antiquae*. While the latter one trusted in the reasonability of God and creation, the modernists stressed God's will and power. In their arguments, they made bright use of logical conclusions and critical analysis of language.

**102.** This is a central distinction in Luther's thoughts, which is not identical with the distinction of the Old and New Testaments. Law and gospel are two kinds of the word of God, spread out in both Testaments. The law in its theological use shows the sin of human beings; the gospel gives the promise that the sinner will be redeemed.

---

*a*    In Latin, *nolle*, meaning "to not want," "to not wish to pursue," etc., opposite to "want."

evils of the world, the human will must be able to will both death and its own perdition. Indeed, it can will everything when it can will the word and work of God; for how can there be anything anywhere that is below, above, within, or without the word and work of God, except God alone?[103] But what is left here to grace and the Holy Spirit? This plainly means attributing divinity to free choice, since to will the law and the gospel, to unwill sin and to will death, belongs to divine power alone, as Paul says in more than one place.

Clearly then, no one since the Pelagians[104] has written more correctly about free choice than Erasmus! For we have said above that free choice is a divine term and signifies a divine power, although no one has yet attributed this power to free choice except the Pelagians; for the Sophists, whatever they may think, certainly speak very differently. Erasmus, however, far outdoes even the Pelagians, for they attribute this divinity to the whole of free choice, but Erasmus only to half of it. They reckon with two parts of free choice—the power of discerning and the power of selecting—one of which they attach to reason, the other to the will, as the Sophists also do. But Erasmus neglects the power of discerning and extols only the power of selecting. So it is a crippled and only half-free choice that he deifies. What do you think he would have done if he had set about describing the whole of free choice?

But not content with this, he outdoes the philosophers too. For with them it is not yet finally settled whether anything can set itself in motion,[105] and on this point the Platonists and Peripatetics[106] disagree throughout the entire range of philosophy. But as Erasmus sees it, free choice not only moves itself by its own power, but also applies itself to things which are eternal, that is, incomprehensible to itself. Here is truly a novel and unprecedented definer of free choice, who leaves Pelagians, Sophists, and everyone else far behind! Nor is that enough for him; for he does not spare even himself, but is more at cross-purposes with himself than with all the rest. For he had previously said that the human will was completely ineffectual without grace (unless he said this in jest), but here where he is giving a serious definition, he says that the human will possesses this power by which it is capable of applying itself to the things that belong to eternal salvation, that is, to things that are incomparably beyond that power. So in this part Erasmus even surpasses himself as well.

**103.** Replacing *himself.*

**104.** "The followers of the British monk, Pelagius, who taught in Rome c. 400 CE and from 412/413 in Palestine. Pelagius denied original or inherited sin, and he held that humans have at all times the freedom to choose between good and evil; the only grace one needs is the knowledge of God's will and commandment. The Pelagian teaching was condemned as heretical at the Council of Ephesus in 431 CE. Luther is of course completely unjust in accusing Erasmus of this sort of heresy" (LW 33:107 n. 9).

**105.** Actually, in Aristotelian thinking, motion had to be caused by something extrinsic. This conviction was included in one of the main arguments of Thomas Aquinas (1225-1274) for the existence of God: going logically back in the line of moving things, Thomas pointed to the "unmoveable mover" as the origin.

**106.** The Aristotelians.

Do you see, my dear Erasmus, that with this definition you put yourself on record (unwittingly, I presume) as understanding nothing at all of these things, or as writing about them quite thoughtlessly and contemptuously, unaware of what you are saying or affirming? And as I said above, you say less and attribute more to free choice than all the others, in that you describe only part and not the whole of free choice and yet attribute everything to it. Far more tolerable is the teaching of the Sophists, or at least of their father, Peter Lombard,[107] when they say that free choice is the capacity for discerning and then also choosing the good if grace is present, but evil if grace is absent. Lombard clearly thinks with Augustine that free choice by its own power alone can do nothing but fall and is capable only of sinning, which is why Augustine, in his second book against Julian,[108] calls it an enslaved rather than a free choice.

You, however, make free choice equally potent in both directions, in that it is able by its own power, without grace, both to apply itself to the good and to turn away from the good. You do not realize how much you attribute to it by this pronoun "itself"—its very own self!—when you say it can "apply itself"; for this means that you completely exclude the Holy Spirit with all his power, as superfluous and unnecessary. Your definition is therefore to be condemned even by the standards of the Sophists, who if only they were not so enraged by blind envy of me, would be rampaging instead against your book. As it is, since it is Luther you are attacking, everything you say is holy and catholic, even if you contradict both yourself and them, so great is the endurance of saintly human beings.

I do not say this because I approve the view of the Sophists regarding free choice, but because I consider it more tolerable than that of Erasmus, since they come nearer the truth. For although they do not say, as I do, that free choice is nothing, yet when they (and particularly the Master of the Sentences[109]) say that it can do nothing without grace, they take sides against Erasmus. [. . .]

### [Ecclesiasticus 15:14-17.
### The Foolishness of Reason]

Now let us turn to the passage from Ecclesiasticus and compare with it, too, that first "probable" opinion. The opinion says that

---

**107.** Peter Lombard (c. 1096–1164) had collected and arranged the *Sentences* of the Teachers of the Church in the twelfth century. This book had become the common textbook for European theology, up to the early days of Luther, who commented on it in his Erfurt times.

**108.** Augustine, *Contra Iulianum*. Augustine's adversary here was Julian of Aeclanum (d. c. 455), holding a position similar to that of Pelagius.

**109.** Referring to Lombard.

free choice cannot will good, but the passage from Ecclesiasticus is cited to prove that free choice is something and can do something. The opinion that is to be confirmed by Ecclesiasticus, therefore, states one thing and Ecclesiasticus is cited in confirmation of another. It is as if someone set out to prove that Christ was the Messiah, and cited a passage that proved that Pilate was governor of Syria, or something else equally wide of the mark. That is just how free choice is proved here, not to mention what I pointed out above, that nothing is clearly and definitely said or proved as to what free choice is or can do. But it is worthwhile to examine this whole passage.

First it says, "God made human beings from the beginning." Here it speaks of the creation of man, and says nothing as yet either about free choice or about precepts. Then follows: "And left them in the hand of their own counsel." What have we here? Is free choice set up here? But not even here is there any mention of precepts, for which free choice is required, nor do we read anything on this subject in the account of the creation of man. If anything is meant, therefore, by "the hand of their own counsel," it is rather as we read in Genesis, chapters 1–2, that the human being was appointed lord of things, so as to exercise dominion over them freely, as Moses says: "Let us make a human being, and let them preside over the fish of the sea" [Gen. 1:26]. Nor can anything else be proved from those words. For in that state, human being was able to deal with things according to one's own choice, in that they were subject to him; and this is called a human counsel, as distinct from God's counsel. But then, after saying that human beings were thus made and left in the hand of their own counsel, it goes on. "God added God's commandments and precepts." What did God add them to? Surely the counsel and choice of human beings, and over and above the establishing of human beings' dominion over the rest of the creatures. And by these precepts God took away from human beings the dominion over one part of the creatures (for instance, over the tree of the knowledge of good and evil) and willed rather that they should not be free.

Then, however, when the precepts have been added, he comes to human being's choice in relation to God and the things of God: "If you want to observe the commandments, they shall preserve you," etc. It is therefore at this point, "If you want," that the question of free choice arises. We thus learn from Ecclesiasticus

**110.** The following shows Luther's attempt to avoid pure and total determinism.

that the human beings are divided between two kingdoms,[110] in one of which they are directed by their own choice and counsel, apart from any precepts and commandments of God, namely, in their dealings with the lower creatures. Here human beings reign and are the lord, as having been left in the hand of their own counsel. Not that God so leaves the human beings as not to cooperate with them in everything, but God has granted them the free use of things according to their own choice, and has not restricted them by any laws or injunctions. By way of comparison one might say that the gospel has left us in the hand of our own counsel, to have dominion over things and use them as we wish; but Moses and the pope have not left us to that counsel, but have coerced us with laws and have subjected us rather to their own choice.

In the other kingdom, however, human beings are not left in the hand of their own counsel, but are directed and led by the choice and counsel of God, so that just as in their own kingdom they are directed by their own counsel, without regard to the precepts of another, so in the kingdom of God they are directed by the precepts of another without regard to their own choice. And this is what Ecclesiasticus means by: "He added his precepts and commandments. If you will," etc.

If, then, these things are sufficiently clear, we have gained our point that this passage of Ecclesiasticus is evidence, not for, but against free choice, since by it human beings are subjected to the precepts and choice of God, and withdrawn from their own choice. If they are not sufficiently clear, at least we have made the point that this passage cannot be evidence in favor of free choice, since it can be understood in a different sense from theirs, namely in ours, which has just been stated, and which is not absurd but entirely sound and in harmony with the whole tenor of Scripture, whereas theirs is at variance with Scripture as a whole and is derived from this one passage alone, in contradiction to it. We stand, therefore, quite confidently by the good sense that the negative of free choice makes here, until they confirm their strained and forced affirmative.

When, therefore, Ecclesiasticus says: "If you will observe the commandments and keep acceptable fidelity, they shall preserve you," I do not see how free choice is proved by these words. For the verb is in the subjunctive mood ("If you will"), which asserts nothing. As the logicians say, a conditional asserts nothing indicatively: for example, "If the devil is God, it is right to worship God; if an ass flies, an ass has wings; if free choice exists, grace is nothing." Ecclesiasticus, however, should have spoken as follows, if he had wished to assert free choice: "Human beings can keep the commandments of God," or: "Human beings have the power to keep the commandments." [. . .]

## [Erasmus's Failure to Distinguish between Law and Gospel]

In these passages our *Diatribe* makes no distinction whatever between expressions of the law and of the gospel; for she is so blind and ignorant that she does not know what law and gospel are.[111] For out of the whole of Isaiah, apart from that one verse, "If you are willing," she quotes not a single word of the law, all the rest being gospel passages, in which the brokenhearted and afflicted are called to take comfort from a word of proffered grace. But Diatribe turns them into words of law. Now, I ask you, what good will anyone do in a matter of theology or the Holy Scriptures, who has not yet got as far as knowing what the law and what the gospel is, or if one knows, nevertheless disdains to observe the distinction between them? Such a person is bound to confound everything—heaven and hell, life and death—and will take no pains to know anything at all about Christ. On this subject I will admonish, dear Diatribe, more fully below.

Look at those words from Jeremiah and Zechariah: "If you return, I will restore you" and "Return to me, and I will return to you." Does it follow from "Return" that you are therefore able to return? Does it follow from "Love the Lord your God with all your heart" that you will therefore be able to love him with all your heart? What, then, do arguments of this kind prove, unless that free choice does not need the grace of God but can do everything in its own strength? How much more correctly, therefore, are the words taken as they stand? "If you shall return, I also will restore you"; that is, if you leave off sinning, I also will leave off punishing you, and if after returning you live a good life, I also will do good to you by turning away your captivity and all your ills. But it does not follow from this that human beings return by their own power, nor do the words themselves say so, but they say simply: "If you return," by which human beings are told what they ought to do; and once God knew this and saw that they

**111.** Here Luther brings forth his fundamental distinction in the word of God: the law, expressing God's will, and the gospel, bringing God's promises even to the sinner.

could not do it, human beings would seek the means enabling them to do it, if Diatribe's leviathan (that is, her added comment and inference) did not intervene to say: "But it would be meaningless to say, 'Return,' if human beings could not return by their own power." What sort of notion that is, and what it implies, has already been sufficiently stated.

Only a human being in a stupor or a daze of some sort could suppose that the power of free choice is established by words such as "Return" and "If you return" without noticing that on the same principle it would also be established by the saying, "You shall love the Lord your God with all you heart," since the meaning of the one who commands and demands is the same in both cases. The love of God is certainly no less required than our conversion and the keeping of all the commandments, since the love of God is our true conversion. Yet no one tries to prove free choice from the commandment of love, though everyone argues for it from sayings such as "If you are willing"; "If you will hear"; "Return!" If, then, it does not follow from that saying ("Love the Lord thy God with all your heart") that free choice is anything or can do anything, it certainly does not follow from sayings such as "If you are willing"; "If you are obedient"; "Return!" which either demand less or demand it less imperiously than "Love God!"; "Love the Lord!"

Whatever, therefore, can be said against the use of the expression "Love God!" as an argument for free choice, the same can be said against the use of all other verbs of command or demand as arguments for free choice. And what can be said is that by the command to love we are shown the essential meaning of the law and what we ought to do, but not the power of the will or what we are able to do, but rather what we are not able to do; and the same is shown by all other expressions of demand. For it is well known that even the academics, with the exception of the Scotists[112] and the Moderns,[113] affirm that human beings cannot love God with all their heart[114]; and in that case, neither can they fulfill any of the other commandments, since all of them depend on this one, as Christ testifies [Matt. 22:40]. So the fact remains, even on the testimony of the Scholastic doctors, that the words of the law are no evidence for the power of free choice, but show what we ought to do and cannot do. [. . .]

See now how the *Diatribe* treats that famous verse of Ezekiel 18: "As I live, says the Lord, I desire not the death of a sinner, but

**112.** John Duns Scotus (c. 1266–1308), British philosopher and theologian of the Franciscan Order, taught in Oxford, Paris, and Cologne. He was known as *Doctor Subtilis,* "the subtle doctor."

**113.** For Modernists, see n. 101, p. 200.

**114.** In the tradition of the *Via moderna,* some thinkers, notably Gabriel Biel (c. 1420–1495), held that human beings could fulfill God's will in a purely natural "naked" state (*ex puris naturalibus*).

rather that the sinner should turn and live." First, Diatribe says: "In every case the words 'turns away . . . has done . . . has performed . . .' are repeated again and again, in the matter of doing good or evil, and where are those who deny that human beings can do anything?" Notice, please, the remarkable consequence. She was going to prove endeavor and desire on the part of free choice, and she proves a complete act, everything fully carried out by free choice. Where now, I ask you, are those who insist on grace and the Holy Spirit? For this is the subtle kind of way she argues: "Ezekiel says, 'If a wicked human being turns away from all sins and does what is lawful and right, that person shall live' [Ezek. 18:21]; therefore, the wicked human being forthwith does so and is able to do so." Ezekiel intimates what ought to be done, and Diatribe takes it that this is being and has been done, again trying to teach us by a new sort of grammar that to owe is the same as to have, to be required as to be provided, to demand as to pay.

Then she takes that word of sweetest gospel, "I desire not the death of a sinner," etc., and gives this twist to it: "Does the good Lord deplore the death of his people which he himself works in them? If he does not will our death and if we nonetheless perish, it is to be imputed to our own will. But what can you impute to a human being who can do nothing either good or ill?" This is just the song Pelagius sang when he attributed not merely desire or endeavor, but the complete power of fulfilling and doing everything, to free choice. For it is this power that these inferences prove if they prove anything, as we have said, so that they conflict just as violently and even more so with Diatribe herself, who denies that free choice has this power, and claims for it only an endeavor, as they conflict with us who deny free choice altogether. But not to dwell on her ignorance, we will confine ourselves to the point at issue.

It is an evangelical word and the sweetest comfort in every way for miserable sinners, where Ezekiel [Ezek. 18:23, 32] says: "I desire not the death of a sinner, but rather that the sinner may turn and live," like Psalm 28 [30:5]: "For God's anger is but for a moment, and God's favor is for a lifetime." Then there is Psalm 68 [109:21]: "How sweet is your mercy, O LORD" and "For I am merciful" [Jer. 3:12], and also Christ's saying in Matthew 11[:28]: "Come unto me, all you who labor, and I will give you rest," and that in Exodus 20[:6]: "I show mercy to many thousands, to those who love me." What, indeed, does almost more than half of Holy Scripture contain but sheer promises of grace, in which mercy, life, peace, and salvation are offered by God to human beings? And what else do words of promise have to say but this: "I desire not the death of a sinner"? Is it not the same thing to say, "I am merciful," as to say, "I am not angry, I do not want to punish, I do not want you to die, I want to pardon, I want to spare"? And if these divine promises were not there to raise up consciences afflicted with the sense of sin and terrified with the fear of death and judgment, what place would there be for pardon or hope? What sinner would not despair? But just as free choice is not proved by other words of mercy or promise or comfort, so neither is it proved by this one: "I desire not the death of a sinner," etc. [. . .]

For this also must be observed, that just as the voice of the law is not raised except over those who do not feel or acknowledge their sin, as Paul says in Romans 3[:20]: "Through the law comes knowledge of sin," so the word of grace does not come except to those who feel their sin and are troubled and tempted to despair. Thus in all expressions of the law you see that sin is revealed, inasmuch as we are shown what we ought to do, just as you see in all the words of promise, on the other hand, that the evil is indicated under which sinners, or those who are to be lifted up, are laboring. Here, for instance, "I desire not the death of a sinner" explicitly names death and the sinner, that is, the evil that is felt as well as the person who feels it. But in the words "Love God with all your heart," we are shown the good we ought to do, not the evil we feel, in order that we may recognize how unable we are to do that good.

Hence nothing could have been more inappropriately quoted in support of free choice than this passage of Ezekiel, which actually stands in the strongest opposition to free choice. For here we are shown what free choice is like, and what it can do about sin when sin is recognized, or about its own conversion to God; that is to say, nothing but fall into a worse state and add despair and impenitence to its sins, if God did not quickly come to its aid and call it back and raise it up by a word of promise. For God's solicitude in promising grace to recall and restore the sinner is a sufficiently strong and reliable argument that free choice by itself cannot but go from bad to worse and (as Scripture says) fall down into hell, unless you credit God with such levity as to pour out words of promise in profusion for the mere pleasure of talking, and not because they are in any way necessary for our salvation. So you can see that not only all the words of the law stand against free choice, but also all the words of promise utterly refute it; which means that Scripture in its entirety stands opposed to it.

## [God Preached, God Hidden; God's Will Revealed, God's Will Secret]

This word, therefore, "I desire not the death of a sinner," has as you see no other object than the preaching and offering of divine mercy throughout the world, a mercy that only the afflicted and those tormented by the fear of death receive with joy and gratitude, because in them the law has already fulfilled its office and brought the knowledge of sin. Those, however, who have not yet experienced the office of the law, and neither recognize sin nor feel death, have no use for the mercy promised by that word. But why some are touched by the law and others are not, so that the former accept and the latter despise the offered grace, is another question and one not dealt with by Ezekiel in this passage. For he is here speaking of the preached and offered mercy of God, not of that hidden and awful will of God whereby God ordains by God's own counsel which and what sort of persons God wills to be recipients and partakers of the mercy of God preached and offered. This will is not to be inquired into, but reverently adored, as by far the most awe-inspiring secret of the Divine Majesty, reserved for God alone and forbidden to us much more religiously than any number of Corycian caverns.[b]

When now Diatribe pertly asks, "Does the good Lord deplore the death of his people, which he himself works in them?"—for this really does seem absurd—we reply, as we have already said, that we have to argue in one way about God or the will of God as preached, revealed, offered, and worshiped, and in another way about God as God is not preached, not revealed, not offered, not worshiped. To the extent, therefore, that God hides Godself and wills to be unknown to us, it is no business of ours. For here the saying truly applies, "Things above us are no business of ours."

---

*b*    See n. 44 above, p. 166.

And lest anyone should think this is a distinction of my own, I am following Paul, who writes to the Thessalonians concerning Antichrist that he will exalt himself above every God that is preached and worshiped [2 Thess. 2:4]. This plainly shows that someone can be exalted above God as God is preached and worshiped, that is, above the word and rite through which God is known to us and has dealings with us; but above God as God is not worshiped and not preached, but as God is in God's own nature and majesty, nothing can be exalted, but all things are under God's mighty hand.

God must therefore be left alone in this divine majesty, for in this regard we have nothing to do with God, nor has God willed that we should have anything to do with God. But we have something to do with God insofar as God is clothed and set forth in the Word, through which God is offered to us and which is the beauty and glory with which the psalmist celebrates God as being clothed. In this regard we say, the good God does not deplore the death of God's own people which God works in them, but rather deplores the death found in God's people and desires to remove from them. For it is this that God as God is preached is concerned with, namely, that sin and death should be taken away and we should be saved. For "God sent the word and healed them" [Ps. 107:20]. But God hidden in majesty neither deplores nor takes away death, but works life, death, and all in all. For there God has not bound Godself by this word, but has stayed free over all things.

Diatribe, however, deceives herself in her ignorance by not making any distinction between God preached and God hidden,[115] that is, between the word of God and God. God does many things that are not disclosed to us in the word; God also wills many things that God does not disclose as willing in the word. Thus God does not will the death of a sinner, according to God's word, but wills it according to God's inscrutable will. It is our business, however, to pay attention to the word and leave that inscrutable will alone, for we must be guided by the word and not by that inscrutable will. After all, who can direct oneself by a will completely inscrutable and unknowable? It is enough to know simply that there is a certain inscrutable will in God, and as to what, why, and how far it wills, that is something we have no right whatever to inquire into, hanker after, care about, or meddle with, but only to fear and adore.

115. This distinction of the preached or revealed and the hidden God (*Deus praedicatus/revelatus* or *Deus absonditus*) is one of the most widely debated questions in Luther research. While for some theologians, as Albrecht Ritschl, the *Deus absconditus* was the worst idea coming from Luther, others feel obliged to its theological depth. The theological roots seem to lie neither in the Platonic theology of Nicholas of Cusa (1401–1464), who wrote a treatise on *Deus absconditus* (*De deo abscondito*), nor in the *Via moderna*'s distinction of God's absolute and ordained power, but, rather, in the advice of Luther's confessor, Johan von Staupitz, who told Luther not to speculate about God's possibilities, but to trust in Jesus Christ alone. The function of the distinction is to direct faith immediately to the good will of God as shown in Christ and not to speculate about God's dark sides.

It is therefore right to say, "If God does not desire our death, the fact that we perish must be imputed to our own will." It is right, I mean, if you speak of God as preached; for God wills all human beings to be saved [1 Tim. 2:4], seeing God comes with the word of salvation to all, and the fault is in the will that does not admit God, as it says in Matthew 23[:37]: "How often did I want to gather your children, and you did not want!" But why that majesty of God does not remove or change this defect of our will in all human beings, since it is not in human beings' power to do so, or why God imputes this defect to human beings, when they cannot help having it, we have no right to inquire; and though you may do a lot of inquiring, you will never find out. It is as Paul says in Romans 11 [9:20]: "Who are you, to answer back to God?" Let these remarks suffice for that passage of Ezekiel, and let us go on to the rest.[116]

Diatribe next argues that all the exhortations in the Scriptures must be quite pointless, as must also the promises, threats, expostulations, reproaches, entreaties, blessings and curses, and all the swarms of precepts, if it is not in anyone's power to keep what is commanded. Diatribe is always forgetting the question at issue and doing something other than she set out to do, not realizing how it all militates more strongly against herself than against us. For on the basis of all these passages, by the force of the inference that she suggests from the words quoted, she proves a freedom and ability to keep everything, though what she wanted to prove was such a free choice as can will nothing good without grace, and a certain endeavor not ascribable to its own powers. I do not find that such an endeavor is proved by any of the passages quoted, but only that a demand is made regarding what ought to be done. This had already been said too often, were not such repetition necessary because Diatribe so often blunders on the same string, putting off her readers with a useless flow of words.

Almost the last passage she quotes from the Old Testament is that of Moses in Deuteronomy 30[:11ff.]: "This commandment which I command you this day is not above you, neither is it far off. It is not in heaven, that you should say, 'Who can go up for us to heaven, and bring it to us, that we may hear it and do it?' . . . But the word is very near you; it is in your mouth and in your heart, so that you might do it." Diatribe contends that by this passage it is declared not only that what is commanded

116. Regarding predestination, see n. 8, p. 157; n. 60, p. 170; and n. 142, p. 247.

is implanted in us, but also that it is like going downhill, i.e., is easy or at least not difficult. We are grateful for such erudition! If, then, Moses so distinctly announces that there is in us not only a faculty, but also a facility for keeping all the commandments, why are we sweating so much? Why did we not promptly produce this passage and assert free choice on a free field? What need is there now of Christ or of the Spirit? We have found a passage that shuts everyone's mouth, and not only distinctly asserts freedom of choice, but also distinctly teaches that the keeping of the commandments is easy. How foolish it was of Christ to purchase for us at the price of his shed blood the Spirit we did not need, in order that we might be given a facility in keeping the commandments, when we already have one by nature!

Nay, even Diatribe herself must recant her own words, in which she said that free choice could do nothing good without grace. Let her now say instead that free choice possesses such virtue that it not only wills good, but also finds it an easy task to keep the greatest and indeed all the commandments. Look, if you please, at what comes of having a mind out of sympathy with the subject, how it cannot help betraying itself! Is there still any need to confute Diatribe? Who could confute her more thoroughly than she confutes herself? She must be that beast they talk of which eats itself! How true it is that a liar ought to have a good memory!

We have spoken of this passage in our commentary on Deuteronomy,[c] so here we shall be brief; and we shall discuss it without reference to Paul, who has a powerful treatment of it in Romans 10[:6ff.]. You can see that nothing whatever is stated or even suggested by any syllable here about the ease or difficulty, power or impotence, of free choice or of human being in the matter of keeping or not keeping the commandments, except insofar as those who entangle the Scriptures in the net of their own inferences and fancies make them obscure and ambiguous for themselves so as to be able to make of them what they please. If you cannot use your eyes, at least use your ears or feel your way with your hands! Moses says it is "not above you, neither is it far off. It is not in heaven. . . . Neither is it beyond the sea." What is "above you"? What is "far off"? What is "in heaven"? What is

---

c   Cf. WA 14:729–31. The commentary was published in the same year of 1525, when Luther wrote *De servo arbitrio.*

"beyond the sea"? Will they make even grammar and the commonest words obscure for us, till we are able to say nothing certain, just to gain their point that the Scriptures are obscure?

According to my grammar, it is not the quality or quantity of human powers but the distance of places that is signified by these terms. What is meant by "above you" is not a certain strength of will, but a place that is above us. Similarly, "far off," "beyond the sea," and "in heaven" say nothing about any power in human nature, but denote a place at a distance from us, upward, on the right, on the left, backward, or forward. I may be laughed at for making such an obvious point and treating such great individuals to an elementary explanation, as if they were little boys learning their alphabet and I were teaching them to put syllables together. But what am I to do when in so bright a light I see them looking for darkness and earnestly wishing to be blind as they reckon up for us such a succession of centuries, so many geniuses, so many saints, so many martyrs, so many doctors, and with such great authority produce and flaunt this passage of Moses, without ever condescending to examine the syllables of which it consists or to control their own flights of fancy so far as to give a moment's consideration to the passage they are shouting about? Let Diatribe now go on and tell us how it is possible for a single private individual to see what so many public figures, the leading lights of so many centuries, have not seen! For certainly this passage, as even a child could judge, proves them to have been not seldomly blind.

In this engraving from the 1523 publication of Luther's *Das Alte Testament deutsch*, which included the Pentateuch, Moses is depicted as kneeling before God, who appears in the clouds with decorative cherubim resting on columns.

What, then, does Moses mean by these very plain and open words, except that he himself has fulfilled his office as a faithful lawgiver excellently? For he has removed every obstacle to their knowing and keeping clearly before them all the commandments, and left them no room for the excuse that they were unaware of or did not possess the commandments, or had to seek them from elsewhere. Hence if they do not keep them, the fault will lie neither with the law nor with the lawgiver, but with themselves; for since the law is there, and the lawgiver has taught it, there remains no excuse on the grounds of ignorance, but only a charge of negligence and disobedience. It is not necessary, he says, to fetch laws from heaven or from places overseas or a long way off, nor can you pretend that you have not heard of them or do not possess them, for you have them close at hand. You have heard them by God's command through my lips, you have understood them in your heart and have received them as a subject of constant reading and oral exposition by the Levites in your midst, as this very word and book of mine bear witness. All that remains is for you to do them. I ask you, what is here attributed to free choice, beyond the fact that it is required to observe the laws given to it, and that any excuse of ignorance or absence of laws is taken away.

These are just about all the texts which Diatribe quotes from the Old Testament in support of free choice, and when these are dismissed, nothing remains that is not equally dismissed, whether she quotes any more or intends to quote more. For she can quote nothing but imperative or subjunctive or optative expressions, which signify, not what we do or can do (as we have so often told Diatribe in answer to her repeated assertions), but what we ought to do and what is demanded of us, in order that we may be made aware of our impotence and brought to the knowledge of sin. Otherwise, if by the addition of inferences and similes invented by human reason these texts prove anything, they prove this, that free choice consists not simply of some little bit of endeavor or desire, but of a full and free ability and power to do everything without the grace of God, without the Holy Spirit. Hence nothing is further from being proved by all that long, repetitive, and emphatic disputation than what had to be proved, namely, that "probable opinion" whereby free choice is defined as being so impotent that it can will nothing good without grace, but is forced to serve sin, though it possesses an endeavor that must not be ascribed to its own powers—a monstrosity[d] indeed that can do nothing by its own powers, yet has an endeavor among its powers, and consists in a quite obvious contradiction.

---

d   Lat., *monstrum.*

## [New Testament Passages:
## Matthew 23:37—Human Beings Must Not Pry
## into the Secret Will of God]

We come now to the New Testament, where again a host of imperative verbs is mustered in support of that miserable bondage of free choice, and the aid of carnal Reason[117] with her inferences and similes is called in, just as in a picture or a dream you might see the king of the flies[118] with his lances of straw and shields of hay arrayed against a real and regular army of seasoned human troops. That is how the human dreams of Diatribe go to war with the battalions of divine words.

First, there steps forward as a sort of Achilles[119] of the flies that saying from Matthew 23[:37]: "Oh Jerusalem, Jerusalem, how often would I have gathered your children together, and you would not!" If all is determined by necessity, she says, could not Jerusalem rightly reply to the Lord: "Why do you torment yourself with vain tears? If you did not wish us to listen to the prophets, why did you send them? Why impute to us what has been done by your will and our necessity?" That is what Diatribe says. And here is our reply. Let us grant for the moment that this inference and proof of hers is right and good; what in fact is proved by it? The probable opinion which says that free choice cannot will the good? It instead proves that the will is free, sound, and capable of doing everything the prophets have said. But that is not what Diatribe set out to prove.

Indeed, let Diatribe herself reply to the following questions. If free choice cannot will good, why is it blamed for not having given heed to the prophets, to whom as teachers of good things it could not give heed by its own powers? Why does Christ weep vain tears, as if they could have willed what he certainly knows they cannot will? Let Diatribe, I say, acquit Christ of insanity in order to maintain that probable opinion of hers, and our opinion will soon be quit of that Achilles of the flies. This passage from Matthew, therefore, either proves total free choice or it militates just as strongly against Diatribe herself and strikes her down with her own weapon.

We say, as we have said before, that the secret will of the Divine Majesty is not a matter for debate, and the human temerity which with continual perversity is always neglecting necessary things in its eagerness to probe this one, must be called

**117.** This combination of words shows that, for Luther, "carnal" is more a theological qualification than a biological description.

**118.** Luther might not only have in mind the strange image of fighting flies, but it is noteworthy that "Baal Zebub" means "man of the flies," as Luther mentioned in his explanation of Rom. 11:4 in his early lecture on the Romans.

**119.** This Greek hero of the Trojan War was invulnerable except in his heel.

**120.** The *absconditia*, "hiddenness of God in light," is a popular idea in medieval mystical thinking.

off and restrained from busying itself with the investigation of these secrets of God's majesty, which it is impossible to penetrate because he dwells in light inaccessible,[120] as Paul testifies [1 Tim. 6:16]. Let it occupy itself instead with God incarnate, or as Paul puts it, with Jesus crucified, in whom are all the treasures of wisdom and knowledge, though in a hidden manner [Col. 2:3]; for through Christ it is furnished abundantly with what it ought to know and ought not to know. It is God incarnate, moreover, who is speaking here: "I would . . . you would not"—God incarnate, I say, who has been sent into the world for the very purpose of willing, speaking, doing, suffering, and offering to all human beings everything necessary for salvation. Yet Christ offends many, who being either abandoned or hardened by that secret will of the Divine Majesty do not receive him as he wills, speaks, does, suffers, and offers, as John says: "The light shines in the darkness, and the darkness does not comprehend it" [John 1:5]; and again: "He came to his own home, and his own people received him not" [John 1:11]. It is likewise the part of this incarnate God to weep, wail, and groan over the perdition of the ungodly, when the will of the Divine Majesty purposely abandons and reprobates some to perish. And it is not for us to ask why he does so, but to stand in awe of God who both can do and wills to do such things.

No one, I think, will wish to deny that this will concerning which it is said: "How often would I . . ." was disclosed to the Jews before God became incarnate, inasmuch as they are accused of having killed the prophets before Christ, and so of having resisted God's will. For it is well known among Christians that everything done by the prophets was done in the name of the Christ who was to come, concerning whom it had been promised that he should be God incarnate. Hence whatever has been offered to human beings from the beginning of the world through the ministers of the word is rightly called the will of Christ. [. . .]

# [Part IV. Defense of Arguments against Free Choice]

Let the above suffice in answer to the first part of Diatribe, in which she has endeavored to establish free choice. Let us now look at the latter part, in which our arguments—i.e., those whereby free choice is abolished—are confuted. Here you will see what human-made smoke can do against the thunder and lightning of God!

First, after having marshaled innumerable passages of Scripture like a very formidable army in support of free choice (in order to inspire courage in the confessors and martyrs and all the saints of both sexes on the side of free choice, and fear and trembling in all those who deny and sin against free choice), she pretends there is only a contemptible little rabble against free choice, and actually allows only two passages, which are more conspicuous than the rest, to stand on this side, she being intent, of course, only on slaughtering them, and that without much trouble. One of these is Exodus 9[:12]: "The LORD hardened the heart of Pharaoh," and the other, Malachi 1[:2f.]: "Jacob I loved, but Esau I hated." Paul explains both of them at some length in the epistle to the Romans [9:11-21], but in Diatribe's judgment it is surprising that he should have engaged in such a distasteful and unprofitable discussion. Indeed, if the Holy Spirit did not know a little about rhetoric, there was a risk of his being shattered by such an artfully managed show of contempt, so that despairing altogether of the cause he would yield the palm to free choice before the bugle blew. But later on I as a mere reservist will with those two passages let our forces also be seen, although where the fortune of battle is such that one can put ten thousand to flight there is no need of any forces. For if any one text defeats free choice, its numberless forces will profit it nothing.

## [Erasmus's Use of Tropes
## in Interpreting Scripture]

Here, then, Diatribe has discovered a new method of eluding the plainest texts by choosing to find a trope[121] in the simplest and clearest words. For just as previously, when she was pleading for free choice, she eluded all the imperative and subjunctive expressions of the law by tacking on inferences and similes, so now, when she is going to plead against us, she twists all the words of divine promise and affirmation in any way she pleases, by discovering a trope in them, so that on both hands she may be an uncatchable Proteus![e] Indeed, she demands in a very haughty

**121.** A trope is a rhetorical type of figurative speech.

e   See n. 124, p. 161.

way that this should be allowed her by us, since we ourselves when we are hard pressed are in the habit of escaping by discovering tropes. For instance, with regard to the text, "Stretch out your hand to whatever you will" [Eccl. 15:16], we say this means "Grace will stretch out your hand to what it wills"; and with regard to, "Get yourselves a new heart" [Ezek. 18:31], we say, "That is, grace will make you a new heart"; and so forth. It seems most unfair, therefore, if it is permissible for Luther to impose such a forced and twisted interpretation that it should not be even more permissible to follow the interpretations of the most highly approved doctors.

You see, therefore, that the controversy here is not about the text itself, nor is it any longer about inferences and similes, but about tropes and interpretations. When, then, are we ever going to have a text pure and simple, without tropes and inferences, for free choice and against free choice? Has Scripture nowhere any such texts? And is the issue of free choice to be forever in doubt because it is not settled by any certain text, but is argued back and forth with inferences and tropes put forward by human beings at cross purposes with one another, like a reed shaken by the wind?*f*

Let us rather take the view that neither an inference nor a trope is admissible in any passage of Scripture unless it is forced on us by the evident nature of the context and the absurdity of the literal sense as conflicting with one or another of the articles of faith.[122] Instead, we must everywhere stick to the simple, pure, and natural sense of the words that accords with the rules of grammar and the normal use of language as God has created it in human beings. For if everybody is allowed to discover inferences and tropes in the Scriptures just as they please, what will Scripture as a whole be but a reed shaken by the wind or a sort of Vertumnus?[123] Then indeed there will be nothing certain either asserted or proved in connection with any article of faith which you will not be able to quibble away with some trope or other. We ought rather to shun as the deadliest poison every trope that Scripture itself does not force upon us.

Look what happened to that master of tropes, Origen, in his exposition of the Scriptures![124] What fitting objects of attack he

**122.** This hermeneutical principle Luther would maintain later on, when facing the Swiss reformer Ulrich Zwingli about the tropological interpretation of the words of institution in the Eucharist.

**123.** The mythological Roman god of seasons, change, and growing fruits and plants. He was able to use his power to change form at will.

**124.** Erasmus himself had introduced this ancient author into the discussion. Origen, in the third century (c. 185–c. 254), widely used the allegorical interpretation of the Scriptures to harmonize it with Neoplatonic theology. To find the philosophy in

*f*  Cf. Matt. 11:7.

provides for the calumnies of Porphyry,[125] so that even Jerome[126] thinks that the defenders of Origen have an impossible task. What happened to the Arians in that trope by which they made Christ into a merely nominal God? What has happened in our own time to these new prophets regarding the words of Christ, "This is my body," where one finds a trope in the pronoun "this," another in the verb "is," another in the noun "body"?[127]

What I have observed is this, that all heresies and errors in connection with the Scriptures have arisen, not from the simplicity of the words, as is almost universally stated, but from neglect of the simplicity of the words, and from tropes or inferences hatched out of men's own heads. [. . .]

the Bible, Origen used the so-called fourfold sense of Scripture. According to this theory, widely used in the Middle Ages, in each Bible passage one finds besides the literal or historical meaning a typological, moral, and eschatological one. The typological sense refers to the principles of faith, the moral one to the deeds of human beings, and the eschatological one to the future of the world in God.

**125.** Porphyry (234–305), with his *Isagoge* ("Introduction"), was one of the most influential philosophical writers of late antiquity in the Middle Ages. Though he was himself a Neoplatonist, nevertheless, he had attacked Origen because of his interpretation of Scripture.

**126.** Generally speaking, Jerome (c. 342–420) was quite skeptical toward Origen.

**127.** Here Luther starts the debate on the Eucharist: Andreas Bodenstein von Karlstadt (1486–1541) was the one who interpreted the word *this* in the sense that not the bread was meant with it, but the lively body of Christ; Zwingli interpreted *is* as "means," and Johannes Oecolampadius (1482–1531) interpreted the noun *body* as a metaphor.

Origen is depicted building a monastic cell with both tools and devotional items nearby. The artist responsible for the design was Maarten De Vos, but the engraving for the volume was done by Johannes Sadeler I (1550–1600) and Raphael Sadeler I, whose surname is at the lower right.

### [Exodus 4:21—The Hardening of Pharaoh's Heart]

Here stands the Word of God: "I will harden Pharaoh's heart" [Exod. 4:21]. If you say this should or can be taken to mean "I will permit it to be hardened," I agree that it can be so taken, and that this trope is widely used in popular speech, as for instance: "I spoiled you, because I did not immediately correct you when you did wrong." But this is not the place for that kind of proof. The question is not whether that trope is in use, nor yet whether it is possible for anyone to make use of it in this passage of Paul, but the question is whether it is safe to use it and certain that it is rightly used in this passage, and whether Paul intended it to be so used. What is in question is not the use another person, the reader, may make of it, but the use the writer, Paul himself, makes of it.

What would you do with a conscience that questioned you like this: "Look, the Divine Author says, 'I will harden Pharaoh's heart,' and the meaning of the verb 'to harden' is plain and well known; but a human reader tells me that 'to harden' in this passage means 'to give an occasion of hardening,' inasmuch as the sinner is not immediately corrected. By what authority, for what reason, with what necessity is the natural meaning of the word thus twisted for me? What if the reader and interpreter should be wrong? What proof is there that this twisting of the word ought to take place in this passage? It is dangerous, and indeed impious, to twist the word of God without necessity and without authority." Will you proceed to help this troubled little soul by saying: "Origen thought so" or "Give up prying into such things, because they are curious and superfluous"? She will reply: "This warning ought to have been given to Moses and Paul before they wrote, and for that matter to God

In this etching published in 1530, Moses and Aaron appear before Pharaoh, but the result is harsher treatment for the Hebrew slaves.

also. What is the point of their worrying us with curious and superfluous sayings?"

This miserable refuge of tropes is thus of no help to Diatribe. Our Proteus must be held fast here until she makes us quite certain that there is a trope in this passage, either by the clearest Scripture proofs or by unmistakable miracles. To the fact that she thinks so, even though it is backed by the toilsome researches of all the centuries, we attach no importance whatever, but continue to insist that there can be no trope here, and that what God says must be taken quite simply at its face value. For it is not for us to decide to make and remake the words of God just as we please; otherwise, what remains in the entire Scripture that would not fit in with Anaxagoras's philosophy,[128] so that anything might be made of anything? I might say, for instance, "God created heaven and earth, i.e., set them in order, but did not make them out of nothing," or "God created heaven and earth, i.e., angels and demons, or the righteous and the ungodly." Who, I ask you, will not in that case become a theologian the moment the book is opened?

Let it be fixed and settled, then, that since Diatribe cannot prove that there is a trope inherent in these texts of ours, which she is trying to water down, she is bound to concede to us that the words must be taken as they stand, even though she might prove that the same trope is extremely common elsewhere, both in all parts of Scripture and in everyone's ordinary speech. On this principle, all the arguments of ours that Diatribe has sought to confute are defended at once, and her confutation is discovered to have absolutely no effect, no power, no reality.

When, therefore, she interprets that saying of Moses, "I will harden Pharaoh's heart," as meaning "My forbearance in tolerating a sinner brings some, it is true, to repentance, but it will make Pharaoh more obstinate in wrongdoing," this is prettily said, but there is no proof that it ought to be said; and we are not content with mere statement, but want proof. Similarly, Paul's saying, "God has mercy on whom God wills, and God hardens whom God wills" [Rom. 9:18], she plausibly interprets as "God hardens when God does not at once punish the sinner, and has mercy as soon as God invites repentance by means of afflictions." But what proof is there of this interpretation? Then there is Isaiah's saying: "You have made us err from your ways, you have hardened our heart, so that we fear you not" [Isa. 63:17].

**128.** According to Aristotle, Anaxagoras, one of the pre-Socratic thinkers, had taught that all things are made out of an innumerous crowd of components that can be combined in manifold different ways.

Granted that Jerome, following Origen, interprets it thus: "One is said to lead astray when one does not at once recall from error," but who can assure us that Jerome and Origen interpret it correctly? In any case, we have an agreement that we are willing to fight each other, not by appealing to the authority of any doctor, but by that of Scripture alone.

Who are these Origens and Jeromes, then, that Diatribe, forgetting our compact, throws at us? For hardly any of the ecclesiastic writers have handled the Divine Scriptures more ineptly and absurdly than Origen and Jerome. To put it in a word, this license of interpretation comes to this, that by a new and unprecedented use of grammar everything is jumbled up, so that when God says, "I will harden Pharaoh's heart," you change the person and take it to mean "Pharaoh hardens himself through my forbearance." "God hardens our hearts" means that we harden ourselves when God delays our punishment. "You, Lord, have made us err" means "We have made ourselves err because you have not punished us." So God's being merciful no longer means that God gives grace or shows compassion, remits sin, justifies, or delivers from evil, but on the contrary, it means that God inflicts evil and punishes!

With these tropes you will end up by saying that God had mercy on the children of Israel when deporting them to Assyria and Babylon, for there God punished sinners, there God invited repentance through afflictions. On the other hand, when bringing them back and liberating them, God did not have mercy on them but hardened them; that is, by God's forbearance and compassion God gave occasion for them to be hardened. In this way, his sending of Christ as Savior into the world will not be said to be an act of mercy on God's part, but an act of hardening, because by this mercy God has given human beings the occasion to harden themselves. On the other hand, by destroying Jerusalem and dispersing the Jews even down to the present day, God is having mercy on them because God is punishing them for their sins and inviting them to repent. When God takes the saints up to heaven on the Day of Judgment, this will not be an act of mercy, but of hardening, inasmuch as it will provide an opportunity for them to abuse God's goodness. But when thrusting the ungodly down into hell, God will be having mercy on them, because God is punishing sinners. I ask you, who ever heard of such acts of divine mercy and wrath as these? [. . .]

. . . God is said to harden when indulging sinners with God's forbearance, but to have mercy when God visits and afflicts them, inviting them to repentance by severity. What, I ask you, did God leave undone in the way of afflicting and punishing Pharaoh and calling him to repentance? Are there not ten plagues recorded? If your definition holds good, that having mercy means punishing and calling the sinner without delay, God certainly had mercy on Pharaoh. Why, then, does God not say, "I will have mercy on Pharaoh" instead of "I will harden Pharaoh's heart"? For in the very act of showing mercy to him, which as you put it means afflicting and punishing him, he says, "I will harden him," which as you put it means, "I will do good to him and bear with him." What more monstrous could be heard? What has now become of your tropes, your Origen, your Jerome? What of your most highly approved doctors whom a solitary individual like Luther is rash enough to contradict? But it is the foolishness of the flesh that compels you to speak like this, for it treats the words of God as a game, not believing them to be meant seriously.

The actual text of Moses, therefore, proves unquestionably that those tropes are worthless fictions in this passage, and that something far other and greater, above and beyond beneficence or affliction and punishment, is signified by the words "I will harden Pharaoh's heart," for we cannot deny that both of those methods were tried in Pharaoh's case with the utmost care and concern. For what wrath and chastisement could have been more prompt than when he was smitten with so many signs and plagues that even Moses himself testifies that there never were any to equal them? Why, Pharaoh himself is moved by them more than once and seems to be coming to his senses, though he is not moved deeply or with abiding results. What forbearance and beneficence, furthermore, could be more generous than when God so readily takes away the plagues and so often remits his sin, so often restores blessings and so often removes calamities? Yet neither is of any avail, and God still says, "I will harden Pharaoh's heart." You see, therefore, even if your ideas of hardening and mercy (that is, your glosses and tropes) are admitted to the fullest extent, as supported by custom and precedent, and such as one can see in the case of Pharaoh, there is still a hardening, and the hardening of which Moses speaks must be of a different sort from that of which you dream. [. . .]

## [How God's Omnipotence Can Be Said to Work Evil]

It may perhaps be asked how God can be said to work evils in us, such as hardening, giving human beings up to their lusts [Rom. 1:24], leading them astray, and so forth. We ought, of course, to be content with the words of God, and believe quite simply what they say, since the works of God are entirely beyond description. Yet in order to humor Reason, which is to say human stupidity, I am willing to be a silly stupid and see whether with a bit of babbling we can in any way move her.

To begin with, even Reason and Diatribe admit that God works all in all [1 Cor. 12:6] and that without God nothing is affected or effective; for God is omnipotent, and this belongs to God's omnipotence, as Paul says to the Ephesians. Now, Satan and human being, having fallen from God and been deserted by God, cannot will good, that is, things which please God or which God wills; but instead they are continually turned in the direction of their own desires, so that they are unable not to seek the things of self. This will and nature of theirs, therefore, which is thus averse from God, is not something nonexistent.[129] For Satan and ungodly human being are not nonexistent or possessed of no nature or will, although their nature is corrupt and averse from God. That remnant of nature, therefore, as we call it, in the ungodly human being and Satan, as being the creature and work of God, is no less subject to divine omnipotence and activity than all other creatures and works of God.

Since, then, God moves and actuates all in all, God necessarily moves and acts also in Satan and ungodly humans. But God acts in them as they are and as found by God; that is to say, since they are averse and evil, and caught up in the movement of this divine omnipotence, they do nothing but averse and evil things. It is like a horseman riding a horse that is lame in one or two of its feet; his riding corresponds to the condition of the horse, that is to say, the horse goes badly. But what is the horseman to do? If he rides such a horse alongside horses that are not lame, this will go badly while they go well, and it cannot be otherwise unless the horse is cured. Here you see that when God works in and through evil persons, evil things are done, and yet God cannot act maliciously although God does evil through evil human beings, because one who is good cannot act maliciously; yet God

129. The traditional Platonic understanding of the evil explained it as the absence of good.

uses evil instruments that cannot escape the sway and motion of God's omnipotence.

It is the fault, therefore, of the instruments, which God does not allow to be idle, that evil things are done, with God setting them in motion. It is just as if a carpenter were cutting badly with a chipped and jagged ax. Hence it comes about that the ungodly human beings cannot but continually err and sin because they are caught up in the movement of divine power and not allowed to be idle, but will, desire, and act according to what kind of persons they are.

All this is settled and certain if we believe that God is omnipotent and also that the ungodly is a creature of God, although as one averse from God and left to God without the Spirit of God, this human being cannot will or do good. The omnipotence of God makes it impossible for the ungodly to evade the motion and action of God, for they are necessarily subject to it and obey it. But this corruption or aversion from God makes it impossible for the creature to be moved and carried along with good effect. God cannot lay aside his omnipotence on account of human beings' aversion, and ungodly human beings cannot alter their own aversion. It thus comes about that human beings perpetually and necessarily sin and err until they are put right by the Spirit of God.

Now in all this, Satan still reigns in peace; under this movement of divine omnipotence, the devil keeps its court undisturbed [Luke 11:21]. Next, however, follows the business of hardening, which can be illustrated thus: The ungodly, as we have said, are like Satan, the prince of the ungodly, in being wholly intent on their own interests; these human beings do not seek after God or care about the things that are God's, but they seek their own wealth, their own glories, works, wisdom, power, and in short their own kingdom, and these they wish to enjoy in peace. But if anyone resists or attempts to encroach upon any of these things, then by the same aversion from God that leads them to seek them, these ungodly human beings are moved to indignation and rage against their adversary and are as incapable of not being angry as of not desiring and seeking; and they are as incapable of not desiring as of not existing, for they are a creature of God, though a vitiated one.

This is the well-known fury of the world against the gospel of God. For by means of the gospel that Stronger One comes who is to overcome the peaceful keeper of the court,[g] and condemns those desires for glory, wealth, wisdom, and righteousness of one's own, and everything in which human beings trust. This provocation of the ungodly, when God says or does to them the opposite of what they wish, is itself their hardening or worsening. For not only are they in themselves averse through the very corruption of their nature, but they become all the more averse and are made much worse when their aversion is resisted or thwarted. So it was when God proposed to wrest ungodly Pharaoh's tyranny from him; God provoked him and increased the hardness and stubbornness of his heart by thrusting at him through the word of Moses, who threatened to take away his kingdom and withdraw the people from his tyranny, without giving him the Spirit inwardly but permitting his ungodly corrupt nature under the rule of Satan to catch fire, flare up, rage, and run riot with a kind of contemptuous self-confidence.

Let no one suppose, therefore, when God is said to harden or to work evil in us (for to harden is to make evil), that God does so by creating evil in us from scratch. [. . .] God works evil in us, i.e., by means of us, not through any fault of God, but owing to our faultiness, since we are by nature evil and he is good; but as God carries us along by God's own activity in accordance with the nature of God's omnipotence, good as God is in God's own being, God cannot help but do evil with an evil instrument, though God makes good use of this evil in accordance with God's wisdom for God's own glory and our salvation.

In this way God finds the will of Satan evil, not because God creates it so, but because it has become evil through God's deserting it and Satan's sinning;[130] and taking hold of it in the course of Satan's working, God moves it in whatever direction God pleases. [. . .]

It is thus that God hardens Pharaoh, when presenting to the ungodly and evil will a word and work which that will hates—owing of course to its inborn defect and natural corruption. And since God does not change it inwardly by the Spirit, but keeps on presenting and obtruding God's words and works from without, while Pharaoh keeps his eye on his own strength, wealth, and power, in which by the same natural defect he puts his

**130.** Here Luther explains the counterposition of God and Satan in a way that is not fully dualistic.

g   Cf. Luke 11:22.

trust, the result is that Pharaoh is puffed up and exalted by his own imagined greatness on the one hand, and moved to proud contempt on the other by the lowliness of Moses and the abject form in which the word of God comes, and is thus hardened and then more and more provoked and exasperated the more Moses presses and threatens him. Now, this evil will of his would not be set in motion or hardened if left to itself, but when the omnipotent Mover drives it along with inevitable motion like the rest of the creatures, it must of necessity will something. Then, as soon as God presents to it from without something that naturally provokes and offends it, it becomes as impossible for Pharaoh to avoid being hardened as it is for him to avoid either the action of divine omnipotence or the aversion or wickedness of his own will. The hardening of Pharaoh by God, therefore, takes place as follows: God confronts his wickedness outwardly with an object that the pharaoh naturally hates, without ceasing inwardly to move by omnipotent motion the evil will which is found there; and Pharaoh in accordance with the wickedness of his will cannot help hating what is opposed to him and trusting in his own strength, until he becomes so obstinate that he neither hears nor understands, but is possessed by Satan and carried away like a raving madman.

If we have carried conviction on this point, we have won our case, and having exploded the human tropes and glosses, we can take the words of God literally, with no necessity to make excuses for God or to accuse God of injustice.[131] [. . .]

### [How God's Foreknowledge Imposes Necessity]

But let us look also at Paul, who takes up this passage from Moses in Romans 9[:15-18]. How miserably Diatribe is tormented here; to avoid losing free choice she twists herself into all sorts of shapes. At one moment she says that there is a necessity of consequence but not of the consequent; at another that there is an ordained will, or will signified, which can be resisted, and a will purposed, which cannot be resisted. At another the passages quoted from Paul are not opposed to free choice, for they are not speaking of a human being's salvation. At another the foreknowledge of God presupposes necessity, while at yet another it does not. At another grace preveniently moves the will to will, accompanies it on its way, and gives it a happy issue. At

**131.** Luther summarizes by saying, "God was quite certain, and announced with utmost certainty, that Pharaoh was to be hardened, because God was quite certain that Pharaoh's will could neither resist the notion of God's omnipotence nor lay outside its own badness nor welcome the introduction of its adversary, Moses" (LW 33:180).

another the First Cause does everything, and at yet another it acts through secondary causes while remaining itself at rest. In these and similar bits of juggling with words, [Diatribe's] only aim is to gain time by distracting our attention for a while from the main issue to something else. She credits us with being as stupid and senseless or as little concerned about the subject as she is herself. Or else, just as little children in fear or at play will put their hands over their eyes and then imagine that nobody sees them because they see nobody, so in all sorts of ways Diatribe, who cannot bear the rays, or rather lightning flashes, of the clearest possible words, pretends that she does not see the real truth of the matter, hoping to persuade us also to cover our eyes so that even we ourselves may not see.

But these are all signs of a mind under conviction and rashly struggling against invincible truth. That figment about the necessity of consequence and of the consequent has been refuted above. Diatribe may pretend and pretend again, quibble and quibble again, as much as she likes, but if God foreknew that Judas would be a traitor, Judas necessarily became a traitor, and it was not in the power of Judas or any creature to do differently or to change his will, though he did what he did willingly and not under compulsion, but that act of will was a work of God, set in motion by God's omnipotence, like everything else. For it is an irrefutable and self-evident proposition that God does not lie and is not deceived. There are no obscure or ambiguous words here, even if all the most learned human beings of all the centuries are so blind as to think and speak otherwise. And however much you are perplexed by it, your own and everyone else's conscience is convinced and compelled to say that if God is not deceived in what God foreknows, then the thing foreknown must of necessity take place; otherwise, who could believe God's promises, who would fear God's threats, if what God promises or threatens does not follow necessarily? Or how can God promise or threaten if God's foreknowledge is fallible or can be hindered by our mutability? Clearly this very great light of certain truth stops everyone's mouth, puts an end to all questions, ensures the victory over all evasive subtleties.

We know, of course, that human foreknowledge is fallible. We know that an eclipse does not occur because it is foreknown, but is foreknown because it is going to occur.[132] But what concern have we with that sort of knowledge? We are arguing about the

132. Indeed, the antic tradition and medieval astronomical tables enabled human beings in early modern times to predict eclipses quite exactly.

foreknowledge of God; and unless you allow this to carry with it the necessary occurrence of the thing foreknown, you take away faith and the fear of God, make havoc of all the divine promises and threatenings, and thus deny God's very divinity. But even Diatribe herself, after a long struggle in which she has tried every possible way out, is at length compelled by the force of truth to admit our view when she says: "The question of the will and the determination of God is more difficult. For God to will and foreknow are the same thing. And this is what Paul means by 'Who can resist God's will if God has mercy on whom God wills and hardens whom God wills?' Truly if there were a king who carried into effect whatever he willed, and nobody could resist him, he could be said to do whatever he willed. Thus the will of God, since it is the principal cause of all things that take place, seems to impose necessity on our will." So says she; and we can at last thank God for some sound sense in Diatribe. [. . .]

Granted foreknowledge and omnipotence, it follows naturally by an irrefutable logic that we have not been made by ourselves, nor do we live or perform any action by ourselves, but by God's omnipotence. And seeing that God knew in advance that we should be the sort of people we are, and now makes, moves, and governs us as such, what imaginable thing is there, I ask you, in us which is free to become in any way different from what God has foreknown or is now bringing about? Thus God's foreknowledge and omnipotence are diametrically opposed to our free choice, for either God can be mistaken in foreknowing and also err in action (which is impossible) or we must act and be acted upon in accordance with God's foreknowledge and activity. By the omnipotence of God, however, I do not mean the potentiality by which God could do many things which God does not,[133] but the active power by which God potently works all in all [cf. 1 Cor. 12:6], which is the sense in which Scripture calls God omnipotent. This omnipotence and the foreknowledge of God, I say, completely abolish the dogma of free choice. Nor can the obscurity of Scripture or the difficulty of the subject be made a pretext here; the words are quite clear and known even to schoolboys, and what they say is plain and easy and commends itself even to the natural judgment of common sense, so that it makes no difference hence how great a tally you have of centuries, times, and persons who write and teach differently.[134] [. . .]

**133.** This was the definition of the absolute power in the *Via moderna*. The Scholastic thinkers referred to it to show the wide range of possibilities God could have realized if God had wanted to do so.

**134.** Luther's argument here focuses on the relationship between God and God's creation: Omnipotence excludes any other power, for example, a human one. And God's foreknowledge in itself includes the knowledge of all future things, so that, in Luther's view, there cannot be any liberty for changing them.

## [Jacob and Esau]

So much for the first passage, which has been about the harden-ing of Pharaoh, but which has in fact involved all the passages and engaged a large part of our resources, invincible as they are. Now let us look at the second, about Jacob and Esau, of whom it was said before they were born: "The elder shall serve the younger" [Gen. 25:23].[135] Diatribe gets round this passage by saying that it "does not properly apply to the salvation of man. For God can will that a human being, willy-nilly, be a slave or a pauper, and yet not so as to be excluded from eternal salvation." I beg you to notice how many sidetracks and bolt-holes a slippery mind will seek out when it runs away from the truth; yet it does not succeed in escaping. Suppose this passage does not apply to the salvation of the human being (though more of this below). Does this mean that Paul achieves nothing by quoting it [Rom. 9:12]? Are we to make out that Paul is ridiculous or inept in so serious a discussion? That is the sort of thing that Jerome does, who with a very superior air, but with sacrilege on his lips, dares in more than one place to say that things have a polemic force in Paul which in their proper contexts they do not have.[h] This is as good as saying that when Paul is laying the foundations of Christian dogma, he does nothing but corrupt the Divine Scrip-tures and deceive the souls of the faithful with a notion hatched out of his own head and violently thrust upon the Scriptures. That is the way to honor the Spirit in Paul, that saint and elect instrument of God! And where Jerome ought to be read with discrimination, and this statement ordered with a good many other impious things which (owing to his halfhearted and dull-witted way of understanding the Scriptures) that gentleman writes, Diatribe drags him [Jerome] in quite uncritically, and without deigning to make things easier by at least an explana-tory comment, treats him as an infallible oracle by which she both judges and modifies the Divine Scriptures. So it is that we take the impious utterances of human beings as rules and norms in interpreting Divine Scripture. And we are still surprised that Scripture should be obscure and ambiguous, and that so many

135. The case of Jacob and Esau was a main argument for the defenders of predestination, because of the use Paul made of it in Rom. 9:13. In his first explanation of the question of predestination, *Ad Simplicianum*, Augustine refers to this extensively.

h   Cf. Jerome, Letter 48,13 *Ad Pammachium*. In his disputation against Scholastic theology, in September 1517, Luther had defended Augustine against the opinion that he would have spoken too harshly.

Teachers of the Early Church should be blind with regard to it when it is treated in this ungodly and sacrilegious manner!

Let therefore the person be anathema who says that things have a polemic force in Paul, which in their proper contexts are not in opposition. For this is only said, not proved, and it is said by those who understand neither Paul nor the passages cited by him, but are misled by taking the words in a sense of their own, that is, in an ungodly sense. For however truly this passage in Genesis 25[:21-23] might be understood of temporal bondage only (which is not the case), yet it is rightly and effectively quoted by Paul to prove that it was not through the merits of Jacob or Esau, but through *the one who calls* that Sarah[136] was told: "The elder will serve the younger" [Rom. 9:11f.]. Paul is discussing whether it was by the virtue or merits of free choice that these two attained to what is said of them, and he proves that it was not, but it was solely by the grace of "God who calls" that Jacob attained to what Esau did not. He proves this, however, by invincible words of Scripture, to the effect that they were not yet born and had done nothing either good or bad [Rom. 9:11]. And the whole weight of the matter lies in this proof; this is what our dispute is all about. [...]

**136.** Luther means Rebekah.

Esau (left), famished by a recent hunting expedition, agrees to sell his birthright to Jacob for a bowl of stew and some bread. Illustration by Pierre Eskrich (c. 1550–c. 1590).

### [The Potter and the Clay]

The third passage [Diatribe] takes up is from Isaiah 45[:9]: "Does the clay say to the one who fashions it, 'What are you making?'" and also Jeremiah 18[:6]: "Like the clay in the potter's hand, so are you in my hand." Again she says that these passages have more polemic force in Paul [Rom. 9:20ff.] than with the prophets from whom they are taken, since in the prophets they refer to temporal affliction, whereas Paul applies them to eternal salvation and reprobation; so that again she insinuates temerity or ignorance in Paul. But before we consider how she proves that neither of these texts excludes free choice, let me first say this, that Paul does not appear to have taken this passage out of the prophets, nor does Diatribe prove that he has. For Paul usually mentions the name of the writer or explicitly states that he is taking something from the Scriptures, and he does neither of these things here. So it is truer to say that Paul is taking this common simile, which others take for other purposes, and using it himself in his own spirit for a purpose of his own, just as he does with the saying, "A little leaven leavens the whole lump," which in 1 Cor. 5[:6] he applies to corrupt morals and elsewhere uses against those who corrupt the Word of God [Gal. 5:9], in the same way as Christ refers to the leaven of Herod and of the Pharisees [Mark 8:15].

No matter, then, how much the prophets may be speaking of temporal affliction (and I refrain from discussing that now, so as to avoid being so often taken up and sidetracked by irrelevant questions), Paul nevertheless uses it in his own spirit against free choice. But as for the idea that freedom of choice is not lost if we are as clay in God's hands when he afflicts us, I do not see the point of it or why Diatribe contends for it, since there is no doubt that afflictions come upon us from God against our will, and put us under the necessity of bearing them willy-nilly, nor is it in our power to avert them, although we are exhorted to bear them willingly. [...]

## [Part V. Rebuttal of Erasmus's Critique of the Assertio]

### [Genesis 6:3 and the Biblical Meaning of "Flesh"]

At length Diatribe comes to the passages cited by Luther against free choice, with the intention of confuting them too. The first of them is Genesis 6[:3]: "My spirit shall not abide in human being forever, for this is flesh." First, she argues that "flesh" here does not mean wicked desire, but weakness. Then she expands Moses' text, to the effect that "this saying does not apply to the whole human race, but only to the human beings of that day," and so it means "in these people." Moreover, it does not apply to all the human beings even of that age, since Noah is excepted. Finally, on the authority of Jerome,[i] she says that in Hebrew this saying gives a different impression, namely, of the clemency and not the severity of God—hoping perhaps to persuade us that since this saying does not apply to Noah but to the wicked, it is not the clemency but the severity of God that applies to Noah, while clemency and not severity applies to the wicked.

But let us leave these frivolities of Diatribe's, who never fails to make it clear that she regards the Scriptures as fables. With Jerome's trifling here we have no concern; it is certain he proves nothing, and we are not discussing Jerome's views but the meaning of Scripture. Let the perverter of Scripture pretend that the Spirit of God signifies indignation. We say he doubly lacks proof. First, he cannot produce a single passage of Scripture in which the Spirit of God stands for indignation, since, on the contrary, kindness and sweetness are everywhere attributed to the Spirit. Second, if he did chance to prove that the Spirit stands for indignation in some place, he still could not prove it to be a necessary consequence that Spirit should be so understood in this passage also. Similarly, he may pretend that flesh stands for weakness, yet he proves just as little. For when Paul calls the Corinthians carnal [1 Cor. 3:3], this certainly does not signify a weakness, but a fault, for he accuses them of forming sects and parties, which is not a matter of weakness or lack of capacity for more solid doctrine, but malice and the old leaven [1 Cor. 5:7f.], which he bids them cleanse out. Let us look at the Hebrew.

"My spirit shall not judge in human beings forever, for they are flesh"—that is what Moses literally says.[137] And if we would only get rid of our own dreams, the words as they stand are, I think, adequately plain and clear. That they are, moreover, spoken by God in wrath is sufficiently shown by what precedes and follows, together with the resultant flood. The reason for Moses' speaking them was that the children of human beings were marrying wives from the mere lust of the flesh, and then so filling the earth with violence that they compelled God in God's wrath to hasten the flood, and only delay for a hundred and twenty years [Gen. 6:3] what God would otherwise never have brought about at all. Read Moses attentively, and you will see plainly that this is what he means. But is there any wonder that the Scriptures are obscure, or that with them you can establish not only a

**137.** Here Luther assumes the traditional understanding of the time that Moses was author of the Pentateuch.

i    Jerome, *Liber quaestionum hebraicorum in Genesim* 6:3.

free but even a divine choice, when you are allowed to play about with them as if you wanted to make a Virgilian patchwork out of them? That is what you call solving problems and removing difficulties by means of an "explanation." But it was Jerome and his master Origen who filled the world with such trifle, and set this pestilent example of not paying attention to the simplicity of the Scriptures.

For me it was enough to find proof in that passage that God called human beings flesh, and so far flesh that the Spirit of God could not abide among them but at an appointed time was to be withdrawn from them. For what God means by saying that the Spirit will not judge among human beings forever, God goes on to explain about setting a limit of a hundred and twenty years during which God will continue to judge. God contrasts "spirit" with "flesh," however, because human beings as being flesh give no admittance to the Spirit, while God being Spirit cannot approve of the flesh, and that is why the Spirit is to be withdrawn after a hundred and twenty years. So you may take Moses' text to mean: "My Spirit, which is in Noah and other holy men, accuses the ungodly by means of the preached word and the life of the godly—for to judge among human beings is to be active among them in the ministry of the word, convincing, rebuking, and exhorting, in season and out of season [2 Tim. 4:2]—but all in vain, because they are blinded and hardened by the flesh, and get worse the more they are judged, just as it always happens when the Word of God comes into the world, that human beings grow worse the more they are instructed. And this has the effect of hastening the wrath, just as the Flood was hastened then, for it not only means that sin is committed but also that grace is despised, and as Christ says: 'When the light comes, human beings hate the light'" [John 3:19].

Since, therefore, on the testimony of God himself, human beings are flesh and have a taste for nothing but the flesh, it follows that free choice avails for nothing but sinning.[138] [. . .] So a Christian should know that Origen and Jerome and all their tribe are perniciously wrong when they deny that flesh stands for ungodly desire in such passages. In 1 Cor. 3[:3], for example, "You are still of the flesh" refers to ungodliness. For Paul means that there are still some ungodly ones among them, and that even the godly, insofar as they have a taste for things carnal, are of the flesh, although they are justified through the Spirit.

**138.** In this passage, *flesh* is meant in a strictly theological sense, contrasted with the divine spirit, not with human mind.

In short, what you will find in the Scriptures is this: Wherever flesh is treated as in opposition to spirit, you can generally take flesh to mean everything that is contrary to the Spirit, as [in John 6:63]: "The flesh is of no avail."[139] But where flesh is treated on its own, you may take it that it signifies the bodily constitution and nature, as for example: "They shall be two in one flesh" [Matt. 19:5]; "My flesh is food indeed" [John 6:55]; or "The Word became flesh" [John 1:14]. In these passages you can drop the Hebraism and say "body" instead of "flesh," for the Hebrew language has only the one word "flesh" for what we express by the two words *flesh* and *body*, and I wish this distinction of terms had been observed in translation throughout the whole canon of Scripture. My passage from Genesis 6, will thus, I think, still stand firmly against free choice, when free choice is proved to be flesh, which Paul in Romans 8[:7] says cannot submit to God (as we shall see in that passage), and which Diatribe herself says can will nothing good. [...]

### [The Whole Human Being—
### Body, Soul, and "Spirit"—Is "Flesh"]

[...] We call ungodly anyone who is without the Spirit of God, for Scripture says it is to justify the ungodly that the Spirit is given. But when Christ distinguishes the Spirit from the flesh by saying: "That which is born of the flesh is flesh," and adds that what is born of the flesh cannot see the kingdom of God [John 3:6, 3], it plainly follows that whatever is flesh is ungodly and under the wrath of God and a stranger to the kingdom of God. And if it is a stranger to the kingdom and Spirit of God, it necessarily follows that it is under the kingdom and spirit of Satan, since there is no middle kingdom between the kingdom of God and the kingdom of Satan, which are mutually and perpetually in conflict with each other. These are the facts that prove that the loftiest virtues of the heathen, the best things in the philosophers, the most excellent things in human beings, which in the eyes of the world certainly appear to be, as they are said to be, honorable and good, are nonetheless in the sight of God truly flesh and subservient to the kingdom of Satan; that is to say, they are impious and sacrilegious and on all counts bad. [...]

139. This biblical passage, a little later, would become central in the debate with Zwingli over the Last Supper. The Zurich reformer used it to deny the real presence of Christ's body in the Eucharist.

## [Divine Grace and Human Cooperation]

[. . .] We are not discussing what we can do through God's working, but what we can do of ourselves; that is to say, whether, created as we are out of nothing,[140] we do or attempt to do anything under the general motion of omnipotence to prepare ourselves for the new creation of the Spirit. Here an answer should have been given, instead of changing the subject. For the answer we give is this: [1] Before human beings are created and are human beings, they neither do nor attempt to do anything toward becoming a creature, and after human beings are created, they neither do nor attempt to do anything toward remaining a creature, but both of these things are done by the sole will of the omnipotent power and goodness of God, who creates and preserves us without our help; but God does not work in us without us, because it is for this God has created and preserved us, that God might work in us and we might cooperate with God, whether outside his kingdom through God's general omnipotence, or inside his kingdom by the special virtue of God's Spirit. [2] In just the same way (our answer continues), before human beings are changed into new creatures of the kingdom of the Spirit, they do nothing and attempt nothing to prepare them for this renewal and this kingdom, and when the human being has been recreated they do nothing and attempt nothing toward remaining in this kingdom, but the Spirit alone does both of these things in us, recreating us without us and preserving us without our help in our recreated state, as also James says: "Voluntarily did God bring us forth by the word of his power, that we might be a beginning of God's creature" [James 1:18]— speaking of the renewed creature. But God does not work without us, because it is for this very thing God has recreated and preserves us, that God might work in us and we might cooperate with God. Thus it is through us that God preaches, shows mercy to the poor, comforts the afflicted. But what is attributed to free choice in all this? Or rather, what is there left for it but nothing? And really nothing! [. . .]

## [Erasmus's "Middle Way" Leads Nowhere]

Here we will bring to an end the defense of those arguments of ours which Diatribe has attacked, lest the book grow to an

**140.** With this, Luther adopts the traditional Christian exegesis, interpreting Gen. 1:1 in the sense of a *creatio ex nihilo*.

immoderate length. Any that remain, if they are worth noting, will be dealt with among the things we have to assert. For as to what Erasmus repeats in his Epilogue—that if our view stands, then all the precepts, all the threats, all the promises are in vain and there is no room left either for merits or demerits, rewards or punishments; and it is difficult to defend the mercy or even the justice of God if God damns those who cannot help sinning, besides other unfortunate consequences, which have so disturbed the greatest minds as to throw them quite off balance—with all these we have already dealt above. We neither accept nor approve that middle way which (in all sincerity, I believe) he recommends to us suggesting that we should concede "a tiny bit" to free choice, so that the contradictions of Scripture and the above-mentioned difficulties might be more easily removed; for by this middle way, not only is the issue not settled, but we are no further forward. For unless you attribute absolutely everything to free choice, as the Pelagians*j* do, the contradictions of Scripture remain, merit and reward are abolished, the mercy and justice of God are done away, and all the difficulties remain which we seek to avoid by means of a tiny, ineffectual power of free choice, as we have sufficiently shown above. We must therefore go all out and completely deny free choice, referring everything to God; then there will be no contradictions in Scripture, and the difficulties, if not cured, can be endured.

I beg of you, however, my dear Erasmus, not to believe that I am pursuing this case more out of passion than principle. I will not let myself be accused of such hypocrisy as to think one way and write another, and it is not true, as you suggest, that I have grown so heated in defense of my views as to be now for the first time denying free choice altogether, after having previously attributed something to it—you can show me no such thing in my books, I know. There are theses and treatises of mine in print, in which I have continually asserted, down to the present moment, that free choice is nothing; it is a reality—I used that word then—only in name.[141] It is under conviction of the truth, and as challenged and compelled by the debate, that I have thought and written as I have. As to my having gone about it with some vehemence, I acknowledge the fault, if fault it is; or rather, I greatly rejoice that this testimony is borne to me in the

**141.** Luther does so in his 1518 *Heidelberg Disputation.*

*j*   See n. 104, p. 201.

world in the cause of God. And may God confirm this testimony at the last day! For no one would be happier than Luther to be commended by the testimony of his time that he had been neither slack nor deceitful in maintaining the cause of truth, but had shown quite enough and even too much vehemence. I should then be blessedly out of reach of Jeremiah's word: "Cursed is that human being who does the work of the LORD with slackness" [Jer. 48:10]. [. . .]

# [Part VI.
# A Display of the Forces on Luther's Side]

We have come to the last part of this book, in which, as we promised, we must produce our forces against free choice. But we shall not produce all of them; for who could do that in one small book, when the whole of Scripture, every jot and tittle of it, is on our side? Nor is it necessary; on the one hand, because free choice is already vanquished and prostrate by a twofold conquest—once where we prove that everything Diatribe thought to be in its favor is actually against it, and again where we show that the arguments she sought to refute still stand invincible. On the other hand, even if free choice were not already vanquished, no more than a couple of missiles would be required to lay it low, and that would be enough. For what need is there, when an enemy has been killed by any one shot, to riddle his or her dead body with a lot more? Now, therefore, we shall be as brief as the subject will allow. And out of our numerous armies we will bring forward two high commanders with a few of their battalions, namely, Paul and John the Evangelist.

## [St. Paul:
## Universal Sinfulness Nullifies Free Choice]

This is how Paul, writing to the Romans, enters into an argument against free choice and for the grace of God: "The wrath of God is revealed from heaven against all ungodliness and wickedness of human beings who in wickedness hold back the truth of God" [Rom. 1:18]. Do you hear in this the general verdict on all human beings, that they are under the wrath of God? What else does this mean but that they are deserving of wrath and punishment? He gives as the reason for the wrath, the fact that they do nothing but what deserves wrath and punishment, because they are all ungodly and wicked, and in wickedness hold back the truth. Where now is the power of free choice to attempt anything good? Paul represents it as deserving the wrath of God, and pronounces it ungodly and wicked. And that which deserves wrath and is ungodly, strives and prevails against grace, not for grace. [...]

[...] Shortly before, Paul has said: "The gospel is the power of God for salvation to everyone who has faith, to the Jew first and also to the Greek" [Rom. 1:16]. Here are no obscure or ambiguous words; "to Jews and Greeks" means that to all human beings the gospel of the power of God is necessary in order that they may have faith and be saved from the wrath that is revealed. I ask you, when he declares that the Jews, rich as they are in righteousness, the law of God, and the power of free choice, are without distinction destitute and in need of the power of God to save them from the wrath that is revealed, and when God makes this power necessary for them, does God not deem them to be under wrath? What human beings will you pick out, then, as not liable to the wrath of God when you are obliged to believe that the finest human beings in the world, the Jews and the Greeks, were in that condition? Again, what exceptions will you make among the Jews and Greeks themselves when Paul without any distinction puts them all into one category and brings them all under the same judgment? Must we suppose that among these two most distinguished peoples there were not any who aspired to virtue? Did none of them strive with all the might of their free choice? But Paul pays no attention to this; he puts them all under wrath, declares them all ungodly and wicked. And must we not believe that in similar terms the rest of the apostles, each in his own sphere, consigned all the other nations also to this wrath?

This passage of Paul's, therefore, stands unyielding in its insistence that free choice, or the most excellent thing in human beings—even the most excellent human beings, who were possessed of the law, righteousness, wisdom, and all the virtues—is ungodly, wicked, and deserving of the wrath of God. Otherwise, Paul's whole argument is valueless; but if it is not, then the division he makes leaves no one on neutral ground, when he assigns salvation to those who believe the gospel, and wrath to all the rest, or takes believers as righteous and unbelievers as ungodly, wicked, and subject to wrath. For what he means is this: The righteousness of God is revealed in the gospel as being of faith, so it follows that all human beings are ungodly and wicked. For it would be foolish of God to reveal righteousness to human beings if they either knew it already or possessed the seeds of it. But seeing that God is not foolish and yet reveals to them the righteousness of salvation, it is evident that free choice, even in the highest type of persons, neither possesses nor is capable of anything, and does not even know what is righteous in the sight of God—unless perhaps the righteousness of God is not revealed to the highest type, but only to the lowest, despite Paul's boasting that he is under obligation both to Jews and Greeks, wise and foolish, barbarians and Greeks [Rom. 1:14].

Therefore, Paul in this passage lumps all human beings together in a single mass, and concludes that, so far from being able to will or do anything good, they are all ungodly, wicked, and ignorant of righteousness and faith. [. . .]

### [Free Choice May Do the Works of the Law but Not Fulfill the Law]

In similarly grave terms, this also is said: "No human being will be justified in one's own sight by works of the law" [Rom. 3:20]. This is strong language—"by works of the law"—just as is also "the whole world" and "all the children of humanity." For it should be observed that Paul refrains from mentioning persons and speaks of pursuits, which means that he involves all persons and whatever is most excellent in them. For if he had said that the common people of the Jews, or the Pharisees, or certain ungodly people are not justified, it might have been thought that he had left out some who by the power of free choice and the help of the law were not altogether worthless. But when he condemns the works of the law themselves and makes them impious in the sight of God, it is clear that he is condemning all those whose strength lay in their zeal for the law and its works.

But it was only the best and noblest that were zealous for the law and its works, and that only with the best and noblest parts of themselves, namely, their reason and will. If, therefore, those who exerted themselves in respect of the law and works with the utmost zeal and endeavor both of reason and will—

in other words, with the whole power of free choice, and were assisted besides by the law itself as with divine aid, finding in it instruction and stimulation—if these, I say, are condemned for ungodliness and, instead of being justified, are declared to be flesh in the sight of God, what is there now left in the whole race of human beings that is not flesh and not ungodly? For all are alike condemned who rely on works of the law. For whether they have exercised themselves in the law with the utmost zeal or with only moderate zeal or with no zeal at all does not matter in the least. None of them could do anything but perform works of law, and works of law do not justify; and if they do not justify, they prove their doers ungodly and leave them in this condition; and the ungodly are guilty and deserving of the wrath of God. These things are so clear that no one can utter one syllable against them. [. . .]

But let us appeal to Paul himself as his own best interpreter, where he says in Gal. 3[:10]: "All who rely on works of the law are under a curse; for it is written, 'Cursed be everyone who does not abide by all things written in the Book of the Law, and do them.'" You see here, where Paul is making the same point in the same words as in the epistle to the Romans, that every time he mentions the works of the law he is speaking of all the laws written in the Book of the Law. [. . .]

From all this it is unmistakably plain that for Paul the Spirit is opposed to works of law in just the same way as he is to all other unspiritual things and to the whole gamut of powers and pretensions of the flesh. It is thus clear that Paul takes the same view as Christ, who in John 3[:6] says that everything not of the Spirit is of the flesh, no matter how splendid, holy, and exalted it may be, even including the very finest works of God's law, no matter with what powers they are performed. For there is need of the Spirit of Christ, without whom all our works are nothing else than damnable. It can be taken as settled, then, that by works of the law Paul means not simply ceremonial works, but all the works of the law in its entirety. With this it will also be settled that everything connected with the works of the law is condemned if it is without the Spirit. And one of the things without the Spirit is that very power of free choice—for this is the matter at issue—which is held to be the most outstanding thing a human being has. Now, nothing more excellent can be said of human beings than that they are engaged in works of the law; and Paul is speaking not of those who are engaged in sins and impiety contrary to the law but of these very ones who are engaged in works of the law, that is to say, the best of people, who are devoted to the law, and who, besides the power of free choice, have the help of the law itself to instruct and inspire them. If, therefore, free choice, assisted by the law and occupying all its powers with the law, is of no avail and does not justify, but remains in the ungodliness of the flesh, what may we suppose it is able to do by itself, without the law?

"Through the law," he says, "comes knowledge of sin" [Rom. 3:20]. He shows here how much and how far the law helps. In other words, he shows that free choice by itself is so blind that it is not even aware of sin, but has need of the law to teach it. But what effort to get rid of sin will anyone make who is ignorant of sin? Obviously, he will regard what is sin as no sin, and what is no sin as sin. Experience shows this plainly enough by the way in which the world, in the persons of those whom it regards as the best and most devoted to righteousness and godliness, hates and persecutes the righteousness of God proclaimed by the gospel, calling it heresy, error, and other abusive names, while advertising its own works and ways, which in truth are sin and error, as righteousness and wisdom. With this text, therefore, Paul stops the mouth of free choice when he teaches that through the law sin is revealed to it as to someone ignorant of one's own sin. That is how far he is from conceding to it any power of striving after the good.

Here we have also the answer to that question which Diatribe so often repeats throughout her book: "If we cannot do anything, what is the point of so many laws, so many precepts, so many threats and promises?" Paul here replies: "Through the law comes knowledge of sin." He replies to this question very differently from the way human beings or free choice thinks. He denies that free choice is proved by the law and cooperates with it to produce righteousness; for what comes through the law is not righteousness but knowledge of sin. It is the task, function, and effect of the law to be a light to the ignorant and blind, but such a light as reveals sickness, sin, evil, death, hell, the wrath of God, though it affords no help and brings no deliverance from these, but is content to have revealed them. Then, when human beings become aware of the disease of sin, they are troubled, distressed, even in despair. The law is no help, much less can these human beings help themselves. There is need of another light to reveal the remedy. This is the voice of the gospel, revealing Christ as the deliverer from all these things. [. . .]

[. . .] Paul's words here are absolute thunderbolts against free choice. First: "The righteousness of God is manifested apart from law." This distinguishes the righteousness of God from the righteousness of the law; for the righteousness of faith comes from grace apart from law. The phrase "apart from law" cannot mean anything else but that Christian righteousness exists apart from the works of the law, in the sense that works of law are utterly useless and ineffective for obtaining it, as he says immediately below: "We hold that human beings are justified by faith apart from works of law" [Rom. 3:28], and as he has said above: "No human being will be justified in God's sight by works of the law" [Rom. 3:20]. From all of which it is very clearly evident that all the devoted endeavors of free choice are worth absolutely nothing. For if the righteousness of God exists apart from law and the works of law, must it not much more exist apart from free choice? Especially as the highest aspiration of free choice is to practice moral righteousness, or the works of the law, with the help afforded by the law to its own blindness and ignorance. This expression "apart from" excludes morally good works; it excludes moral righteousness; it excludes preparations for grace. In a word, imagine whatever you may as being within the power of free choice, Paul will still persist in saying that the righteousness of God avails "apart from" that kind of thing. And suppose I allow that free choice can by its own endeavor achieve something—good works, let us say, or the righteousness of the civil or moral law—yet it does not attain to the righteousness of God, nor does God regard its efforts as in any way qualifying it for his righteousness, since he says that his righteousness functions apart from the law. But if it does not attain to the righteousness of God, what will it gain if by its own works and endeavors (if this were possible) it achieves the very sanctity of angels? The words are not, I think, obscure or ambiguous here, nor is there room for any kind of tropes. For Paul clearly distinguishes the two kinds of righteousness, attributing one to the law and the other to grace, maintaining that the latter is given without the former and apart from its works, while the former without the latter does not justify or count for anything. I should like to see, therefore, how free choice can stand up and defend itself against these things.

A second thunderbolt is his saying that the righteousness of God is revealed and avails for all and upon all who believe in Christ, and that there is no distinction [Rom. 3:21f.]. Once more in the plainest terms he divides the entire race of human beings into two, giving the righteousness of God to believers and denying it to unbelievers. Now, no one is crazy enough to doubt that the power or endeavor of free choice is something different from faith in Jesus Christ. But Paul denies that anything outside this faith is righteous in the sight of God; and if it is not righteous in the sight of God, it must necessarily be sin. For with God there is nothing intermediate between righteousness and sin, no neutral ground, so to speak, which is neither righteousness nor sin. Otherwise, Paul's whole argument would come to nothing, since it presupposes this division, namely, that whatever is done or devised among human beings is either righteousness or sin before God: righteousness if faith is present, sin if faith is absent. With men, of course, it is certainly a fact that there are middle and neutral cases, where human beings neither owe one another anything nor do anything for one another. But ungodly human beings sin against God whether eating or drinking or doing whatever, because they perpetually misuse God's creatures in their own impiety and ingratitude, and never for a moment give glory to God from the heart.

It is also no small thunderbolt when he says: "All have sinned and fall short of the glory of God" and "There is no distinction" [Rom. 3:23, 22]. I ask you, could he put it more plainly? Show me a worker of free choice and tell me whether in that enterprise he or she also sins. If there is no sin, why does not Paul make an exception here? Why does he include this worker "without distinction"? It is certain that one who says "all" eliminates no one in any place, at any time, in any work or endeavor. Hence if you exclude any human beings for any kind of effort or work, you make Paul a liar, because the subject of such work and endeavor of free choice is also included in "all" and Paul ought to have had enough respect for him not to place him so freely and without qualification among sinners.

Then there is the statement that they lack the glory of God. You can take "the glory of God" here in two senses, active and passive. This is an example of Paul's habit of using Hebraisms. Actively, the glory of God is that by which God glories in us; passively, it is that by which we glory in God. It seems to me, however, that it ought to be taken passively here—like "the faith of Christ," which suggests in Latin the faith that Christ has, but to the Hebrew mind means the faith we have in Christ. Similarly, "the righteousness of God" in Latin means the righteousness that God possesses, but a Hebrew would understand it as the righteousness that we have from God and in the sight of God. So we take "the glory of God" not in the Latin but in the Hebrew sense as that which we have in God and before God, and which might be called "glory in God." Now, human beings glory in God when they are certain that God is favorable to them and deigns to look kindly upon them, so that the things these human beings do are pleasing in God's sight, or if they are not, they are borne with and pardoned. If, then, the enterprise or endeavor of free choice is not sin, but good in God's sight, it can certainly glory and say with confidence as it glories: "This pleases God, God approves of this, God counts this worthy and accepts it, or at least bears with it and pardons it. For this is the glory of the faithful in God, and those who do not have it are rather put to shame before him." But Paul here denies this, saying that human beings are completely devoid of this glory. Experience proves that he is right; for ask all the exercisers of free choice to a human being, and if you are able to show me one who can sincerely and honestly say with regard to any effort or endeavor of his own, "I know that this pleases God," then I will admit defeat and yield you the palm. But I know there is not one to be found.

Now, if this glory is lacking, so that the conscience dare not say for certain or with confidence that "this pleases God," then it is certain it does not please God. For as human beings believe, so it is with them; and in this case the human beings do not believe with certainty that they please God, although it is necessary to do so, because the offense of unbelief lies precisely in having doubts about the favor of God, who wishes us to believe with the utmost possible certainty that God is favorable. We thus convict them on the evidence of their own conscience that free choice, when it is devoid of the glory of God, is perpetually guilty of the

sin of unbelief, together with all its powers, efforts, and enter-
prises. [...]

### [The Righteousness of Works and of Faith;
### and a Summary of St. Paul's Testimony
### Against Free Choice]

Let us take a look here at what Paul says later about the example
of Abraham [Rom. 4:1-3]. "If Abraham," he says, "was justified
by works, he has something to boast about, but not before God.
For what does the Scripture say? 'Abraham believed God, and it
was reckoned to him as righteousness.'" Please notice here too
the distinction Paul makes by referring to a twofold righteousness of Abraham.

First, there is the righteousness of works, or moral and civil
righteousness; but he denies that Abraham is justified in God's
sight by this, even if he is righteous in the sight of human beings
because of it. With this righteousness, he has indeed something
to boast about before human beings, but like the rest he falls
short of the glory of God. Nor can anyone say here that it is
the works of the law, or ceremonial works, that are being condemned, seeing that Abraham lived so many years before the law
was given. Paul is speaking simply about the works Abraham
did, and the best ones he did. For it would be absurd to argue as
to whether anyone is justified by bad works. If, therefore, Abraham is not righteous because of any works, and if both he himself and all his works remain in a state of ungodliness unless he
is clothed with another righteousness, namely, that of faith, then
it is plain that no human beings are brought any nearer to righteousness by their works; and what is more, that no works and no
aspirations or endeavors of free choice count for anything in the
sight of God, but are all adjudged to be ungodly, unrighteous,
and evil. For if the human beings are not righteous, neither are
their works or endeavors righteous; and if they are not righteous,
they are damnable and deserving of wrath.

The other kind of righteousness is the righteousness of faith,
which does not depend on any works, but on God's favorable
regard and God's "reckoning" on the basis of grace. Notice how
Paul dwells on the word "reckoned," how he stresses, repeats, and
insists on it. "To one who works," he says, "that person's wages
are not reckoned as a gift but as a due. And to one who does not

work but has faith in him who justifies the ungodly, that person's faith is reckoned as righteousness, according to the plan of God's grace" [Rom. 4:4f.]. Then he quotes David as saying the same about the "reckoning" of grace: "Blessed are the human beings against whom the Lord will not reckon their sin," etc. [Rom. 4:6ff.]. He repeats the word *reckon* nearly ten times in this chapter. In short, Paul sets the one who works and the one who does not work alongside each other, leaving no room for anyone between them; and he asserts that righteousness is not reckoned to the former, but that it is reckoned to the latter provided he has faith. There is no way of escape for free choice here, no chance for it to get away with its endeavoring and striving. It must be classed either with the one who works or with the one who does not work. If it is classed with the former, so you are told here, it does not have any righteousness reckoned to it, whereas if it is classed with the latter—the one who does not work but has faith in God—then it does have righteousness reckoned to it. But in that case it will no longer be a case of free choice at work, but of a being created anew through faith.

Now, if righteousness is not reckoned to those who work, then clearly their works are nothing but sins, evils, and impieties in the sight of God. Nor can any impudent Sophist break in here with the objection that human beings' works need not be evil, even if they themselves are evil. For Paul purposely speaks, not simply of the human being as a human being, but of the person as a worker, in order to make it unmistakably plain that human works and endeavors themselves are condemned, no matter what their nature, name, or sign may be. It is, however, with good works that he is concerned, since he is arguing about justification and merit. Hence, although with the phrase "one who works" he refers quite generally to all workers and all their works, it is particularly of their good and virtuous works that he is speaking about. Otherwise, there would be no point in his distinction between the "one who works" and the "one who does not work."

I will not here elaborate the very strong arguments that can be drawn from the purpose of grace, the promise of God, the meaning of the law, original sin, or divine election, any one of which would be sufficient by itself to do away completely with free choice. For if grace comes from the purpose or predestination[142] of God, it comes by necessity and not by our effort or endeavor, as we have shown above. Moreover, if God promised

142. "Predestination" as a determination of human salvation or damnation has to be distinguished from "foreknowledge"/ "prescience," which just means that God knows everything even before determining or not.

grace before the law was given, as Paul argues here and in Galatians, then grace does not come from works or through the law; otherwise the promise means nothing. So also faith will mean nothing—although Abraham was justified by it before the law was given—if works count for anything. Again, since the law is the power of sin [1 Cor. 15:56] in that it serves only to reveal and not to remove sin, it makes the conscience guilty before God and threatens it with wrath. That is what Paul means when he says: "The law brings wrath" [Rom. 4:15]. How, then, could there be any possibility of attaining righteousness through the law? And if we receive no help from the law, what help can we expect from the power of choice alone?

Furthermore, seeing that through the one transgression of the one man, Adam, we are all under sin and damnation, how can we attempt anything that is not sinful and damnable? For when he says "all," he makes no exception either of the power of free choice or of any worker, but every human being, whether working or not, endeavoring or not, is necessarily included among the "all." Not that we should sin or be damned through that one transgression of Adam if it were not our own transgression. For who could be damned for another's transgression, especially before God? It does not, however, become ours by any imitative doing of it ourselves, for then it would not be the one transgression of Adam, since it would be we and not Adam who committed it; but it becomes ours the moment we are born—a subject we must deal with some other time. Original sin itself, therefore, leaves free choice with no capacity to do anything but sin and be damned. [. . .]

. . . In Romans 8[:5], where Paul divides the human race into two types, namely, flesh and spirit (just as Christ does in John 3[:6]), he says: "Those who live according to the flesh set their minds on the things of the flesh, but those who live according to the Spirit set their minds on the things of the Spirit." That Paul here calls carnal all who are not spiritual is evident both from this very partition and opposition between spirit and flesh, and from his own subsequent statement: "You are not in the flesh but in the Spirit if the Spirit of God really dwells in you. Anyone who does not have the Spirit of Christ does not belong to him" [Rom. 8:9]. What else is the meaning of "You are not in the flesh if the Spirit of God is in you" but that those who do not have the Spirit are necessarily in the flesh? And if anyone does not belong to Christ, to whom else does one belong but Satan? Clearly, then, those who lack the Spirit are in the flesh and subject to Satan.

Now let us see what he thinks of the endeavor and power of free choice in those he calls carnal. "Those who are in the flesh cannot please God" [Rom. 8:8]. And again: "The mind of the flesh is death" [v. 6]. And again: "The mind of the flesh is enmity toward God" [v. 7]. Also: "It does not submit to God's law, indeed it cannot" [v. 7]. Here let the advocate of free choice tell me this: how something that is death, displeasing to God, hostility toward God, disobedient to God, and incapable of obedience can possibly strive toward the good? For Paul did not choose to say simply that the mind of the flesh is "dead" or "hostile to God," but that it is death itself, hostility itself, which cannot possibly submit to God's law or please God, just as he had said a little before: "For what was impossible to the law, in that it was weak because of the flesh, God has done," etc. [v. 3].

I, too, am familiar with Origen's fable about the threefold disposition of flesh, soul, and spirit, with soul standing in the middle and being capable of turning either way, toward the flesh or toward the spirit.[143] But these are dreams of his own; he states but does not prove them. Paul here calls everything flesh that is without the Spirit, as we have shown. Hence the loftiest virtues of the best of human beings are in the flesh, that is to say, they are dead, hostile to God, not submissive to the law of God and not capable of submitting to it, and not pleasing to God. For Paul says not only that they do not submit, but that they cannot. So also Christ says in Matthew 7[:18]: "A bad tree cannot bear good fruit," and in Matthew 12[:34]: "How can you speak good when you are evil?" You see here not only that we speak evil, but that we cannot speak good. And although he says elsewhere that we who are evil know how to give good gifts to our children [Matt. 7:11], yet he denies that we do good even when we give good gifts, because although what we give is a good creation of God, we ourselves are not good, nor do we give these good things in a good way; and he is speaking to all people, including his disciples. Thus the twin statements of Paul are confirmed, that the righteous live by faith [Rom. 1:17], and that whatsoever is not of faith is sin [Rom. 14:23]. The latter follows from the former, for if there is nothing by which we are justified but faith, it is evident that those who are without faith are not yet justified; and those who are not justified are sinners; and sinners are

143. With this "tripartite" view of human nature, Origen drew from the Platonic anthropology, trying to combine it with Gal. 5:17. The tripartite view, on the basis of 1 Thess. 5:23; Heb. 4:12; and Gen. 2:7 was supported by, e.g., Irenaeus (c. 130–202), Justin Martyr (c. 100–165), Origen, Gregory of Nyssa (c. 335–394), and Basil of Caesarea (c. 330–379).

"bad trees" and cannot do anything but sin and "bear bad fruit." Hence, free choice is nothing but a slave of sin, death, and Satan, not doing and not capable of doing or attempting to do anything but evil.[144] [. . .]

### [The Two Kingdoms, of Christ and of Satan. The Assurance of Faith]

For Christians know there are two kingdoms in the world, which are bitterly opposed to each other. In one of them Satan reigns, who is therefore called by Christ "the ruler of this world" [John 12:31] and by Paul "the god of this world" [2 Cor. 4:4]. It holds captive to its will all who are not snatched away from him by the Spirit of Christ, as the same Paul testifies, nor does he allow them to be snatched away by any powers other than the Spirit of God, as Christ testifies in the parable of the strong man guarding his palace in peace [Luke 11:21]. In the other kingdom, Christ reigns, and his kingdom ceaselessly resists and makes war on the kingdom of Satan. Into this kingdom we are transferred, not by our own power but by the grace of God, by which we are set free from the present evil age and delivered from the dominion of darkness.[145]

The knowledge and confession of these two kingdoms perpetually warring against each other with such might and main would alone be sufficient to confute the dogma of free choice, seeing that we are bound to serve in the kingdom of Satan unless we are delivered by the power of God. These things, I say, the common people know, and they confess them abundantly in their proverbs and prayers, their attitudes and their whole life. [. . .]

For my own part, I frankly confess that even if it were possible, I should not wish to have free choice given to me, or to have anything left in my own hands by which I might strive toward salvation. For, on the one hand, I should be unable to stand firm and keep hold of it amid so many adversities and perils and so many assaults of demons, seeing that even one demon is mightier than all men, and no human being at all could be saved; and on the other hand, even if there were no perils or adversities or demons, I should nevertheless have to labor under perpetual uncertainty and to fight as one beating the

**144.** See also *The Freedom of a Christian*, LW 31:327–378, and TAL, vol. 1, pp. 464–538.

**145.** The famous doctrine of the two kingdoms or of the two regiments was introduced by Luther in his tract about government (*Obrigkeitsschrift*) in 1523. The basic idea is that all human beings are divided up into the kingdom of Jesus Christ and the kingdom of the world or of Satan, as described above. To maintain order in the world and to bring about salvation, God has established two regiments: on the one hand, God reigns by means of the law in its political use, preventing human beings from sin. This regiment is mainly performed by the government. On the other hand, law in its theological use and gospel are preached in the church to redeem all those who come to faith.

air, since even if I lived and worked to eternity, my conscience would never be assured and certain how much it ought to do to satisfy God. For whatever work might be accomplished, there would always remain an anxious doubt whether it pleased God or whether God required something more, as the experience of all self-justifiers proves, and as I myself learned to my bitter cost through so many years.[146] But now, since God has taken my salvation out of my hands into God's hands, making it depend on God's choice and not mine, and has promised to save me, not by my own work or exertion but by God's grace and mercy, I am assured and certain both that God is faithful and will not lie to me, and also that God is too great and powerful for any demons or any adversities to be able to break God or to snatch me from God. "No one," Christ says, "shall snatch them out of my hand, because my Father who has given them to me is greater than all" [John 10:28f.]. So it comes about that, if not all, some and indeed many are saved, whereas by the power of free choice none at all would be saved, but all would perish together. Moreover, we are also certain and sure that we please God, not by the merit of our own working, but by the favor of God's mercy promised to us, and that if we do less than we should or do it badly, God does not hold this against us, but in a parental[k] way pardons and corrects us. Hence the glorying of all the saints in their God.

## [The Mercy and Justice of God in the Light of Nature, Grace, and Glory]

Now, if you are disturbed by the thought that it is difficult to defend the mercy and justice of God who damns the undeserving, that is to say, ungodly human beings who are what they are because they were born in ungodliness and can in no way help being and remaining ungodly and damnable, but are compelled by a necessity of nature to sin and to perish (as Paul says: "We were all children of wrath like the rest" [Eph. 2:3], since they are created so by God from seed corrupted by the sin of the one man Adam)—rather must God be honored and revered as supremely merciful toward those whom God justifies and saves,

146. In a personal retrospect, written as a preface to the 1545 edition of his Latin works, Luther wrote of his agony and discovery: "Though I lived as a monk without reproach, I felt that I was a sinner before God with an extremely disturbed conscience. . . . I did not love, yes, I hated the righteous God who punishes sinners . . . I was angry with God. . . . I raged with a fierce and troubled conscience. . . . At last, by the mercy of God, meditating day and night I gave heed to the context of the words, namely, 'In it the righteousness of God is revealed,' as it is written, 'He who through faith is righteous shall live.' . . . There I began to understand that by which the righteous lives by a gift of God, namely, by faith. And this is the meaning: the righteousness of God is revealed by the gospel, namely, the passive righteousness with which merciful God justifies us by faith, as it is written, 'He who through faith is righteous shall live.' Here I felt that I was altogether born again and had entered paradise itself through open gates. There a totally other face of the entire Scripture showed itself to me" (LW 34:336-37).

---

k    The Latin text here has *Paterne*, which means "fatherly."

supremely unworthy as they are, and there must be at least some acknowledgment of God's divine wisdom so that God may be believed to be righteous where God seems to us to be unjust. For if God's righteousness were such that it could be judged to be righteous by human standards, it would clearly not be divine and would in no way differ from human righteousness. But since God is the one true God, and is wholly incomprehensible and inaccessible to human reason, it is proper and indeed necessary that God's righteousness also should be incomprehensible, as Paul also says where he exclaims: "Oh the depth of the riches of the wisdom and the knowledge of God! How incomprehensible are his judgments and how unsearchable his ways!" [Rom 11:33]. But they would not be incomprehensible if we were able in every instance to grasp how they are righteous. What is a human being compared with God? How much is there within our power compared with God's power? What is our strength in comparison with God's resources? What is our knowledge compared with God's wisdom? What is our substance over against God's substance? In a word, what is our all compared with God's?

If, therefore, we confess, as even nature teaches, that human power, strength, wisdom, substance, and everything we have is simply nothing at all in comparison with divine power, strength, wisdom, knowledge, and substance, what is this perversity that makes us attack God's righteousness and judgment only, and make such claims for our own judgment as to wish to comprehend, judge, and evaluate the divine judgment? Why do we

A statue of Pliny the Younger on the façade
of the Cathedral of St. Maria Maggiore in Como.

not take a similar line here too, and say, "Our judgment is nothing in comparison with the divine judgment"? Ask Reason herself whether she is not convinced and compelled to confess that she is foolish and rash in not allowing the judgment of God to be incomprehensible when she admits that everything else divine is incomprehensible. In all other matters we grant God the divine majesty that belongs to God alone, and only in respect of God's judgment are we prepared to deny it. We cannot for a while believe that God is righteous, even though God has promised us that when God's glory is revealed, we shall all both see and feel that God has been and is righteous.

I will give an example to confirm this faith and console that evil eye which suspects God of injustice. As you can see, God so orders this corporal world in its external affairs that if you respect and follow the judgment of human reason, you are bound to say either that there is no God or that God is unjust. As the poet says: "Oft I am moved to think there are no gods!"[I] For look at the prosperity the wicked enjoy and the adversity the good endure, and note how both proverbs and that parent of proverbs, experience, testify that the bigger the scoundrel the greater his luck. "The tents of the ungodly are at peace," says Job [12:6], and Ps. 72 [73:12] complains that the sinners of the world increase in riches. Tell me, is it not in everyone's judgment most unjust that the wicked should prosper and the good suffer? But that is the way of the world. Here even the greatest minds have stumbled and fallen, denying the existence of God and imagining that all things are moved at random by blind Chance or Fortune. So, for example, did the Epicureans and Pliny;[147] while Aristotle, in order to preserve his Supreme Being from unhappiness, never lets this Being look at anything but itself, because he thinks it would be most unpleasant for it to see so much suffering and so many injustices. The prophets, however, who did believe in God, had more temptation to regard God as unjust—Jeremiah, for instance, and Job, David, Asaph, and others. What do you suppose Demosthenes and Cicero thought,[148] when after doing all they could they were rewarded with so tragic a death?

**147.** Pliny the Younger (61–c. 113) had presented his philosophical ideas in his letters, many of which still survive.

**148.** Demosthenes committed suicide; Cicero was murdered.

*I*   Ovidius, *Amores* 3,9,36.

Yet all this, which looks so very like injustice in God, and which has been represented as such with arguments that no human reason or light of nature can resist, is very easily dealt with in the light of the gospel and the knowledge of grace, by which we are taught that although the ungodly flourish in their bodies, they lose their souls. In fact, this whole insoluble problem finds a quick solution in one short sentence, namely, that there is a life after this life, and whatever has not been punished and rewarded here will be punished and rewarded there, since this life is nothing but an anticipation, or rather, the beginning of the life to come.

If, therefore, the light of the gospel, shining only through the Word and faith, is so effective that this question which has been discussed in all ages and never solved is so easily settled and put aside, what do you think it will be like when the light of the Word and of faith comes to an end, and reality itself and the Divine Majesty are revealed in their own light? Do you not think that the light of glory will then with the greatest of ease be able to solve the problem that is insoluble in the light of the Word or of grace, seeing that the light of grace has so easily solved the problem that was insoluble in the light of nature?

Let us take it that there are three lights—the light of nature, the light of grace, and the light of glory, to use the common and valid distinction. By the light of nature, it is an insoluble problem how it can be just that a good human being should suffer and a bad human being prosper; but this problem is solved by the light of grace. By the light of grace it is an insoluble problem how God can damn one who is unable by any power of his own to do anything but sin and be guilty. Here both the light of nature and the light of grace tell us that it is not the fault of the unhappy person, but of an unjust God; for they cannot judge otherwise of a God who crowns one ungodly human being freely and apart from merits, yet damns another who may well be less, or at least not more, ungodly. But the light of glory tells us differently, and it will show us hereafter that the God whose judgment here is one of incomprehensible righteousness is a God of most perfect and manifest righteousness. In the meantime, we can only *believe* this, being admonished and confirmed by the example of the light of grace, which performs a similar miracle in relation to the light of nature.

# [Conclusion]

## [That the Case against Free Choice Is Unanswerable Let Erasmus Be Willing to Admit]

I will here bring this little book to an end, though I am prepared if need be to carry the debate further. However, I think quite enough has been done here to satisfy the godly and anyone who is willing to admit the truth without being obstinate. For if we believe it to be true that God foreknows and predestines all things, that God can neither be mistaken in divine foreknowledge nor hindered in God's predestination, and that nothing takes place but as God wills it (as reason itself is forced to admit), then on the testimony of reason itself there cannot be any free choice in human being or angel or any creature.

Similarly, if we believe that Satan is the ruler of this world, who is forever plotting and fighting against the kingdom of Christ with all its powers, and that Satan will not let human beings go who are its captives unless they are forced to do so by the divine power of the Spirit, then again it is evident that there can be no such thing as free choice.

Similarly, if we believe that original sin has so ruined us that even in those who are led by the Spirit it causes a great deal of trouble by struggling against the good, it is clear that in a human being devoid of the Spirit there is nothing left that can turn toward the good, but only toward evil.

Again, if the Jews, who pursued righteousness to the utmost of their powers, rather ran headlong into unrighteousness, while the Gentiles, who pursued ungodliness, attained righteousness freely and unexpectedly, then it is also manifest from this very fact and experience that human beings without grace can will nothing but evil.

To sum up: If we believe that Christ has redeemed human beings by his blood, we are bound to confess that the whole human being was lost; otherwise, we should make Christ either superfluous or the redeemer of only the lowest part of humanity, which would be blasphemy and sacrilege.

My dear Erasmus, I beg you now for Christ's sake to do at last as you promised; for you promised you would willingly yield to anyone who taught you better. Have done with respecting of persons! I recognize that you are a great man, richly endowed with the noblest gifts of God—with talent and learning, with eloquence bordering on the miraculous, to mention no others—while I have and am nothing, unless I may venture to boast that I am a Christian. Moreover, I praise and commend you highly for this also, that unlike all the rest, you alone have attacked the real issue, the essence of the matter in dispute, and have not wearied me with irrelevancies about the papacy, purgatory, indulgences, and such like trifles (for trifles they are rather than basic issues), with which almost everyone hitherto has gone hunting for me without success. You and you alone have seen the question on which everything hinges, and have aimed at the vital spot, for which I sincerely thank you, since I am only too glad to give as much attention to this subject as time and leisure permit. If those who have attacked me hitherto had done the same, and if those who now boast of new spirits and new revelations would still do it, we should have less of sedition and sects and more of peace and concord. But God has in this way through Satan punished our ingratitude.

Unless, however, you can conduct this case differently from the way you have in this diatribe, I could very much wish that you would be content with your own special gift, and would study, adorn, and promote languages and literature as you have hitherto done with great profit and distinction. I must confess that in this direction you have done no small service to me too, so that I am considerably indebted to you, and in this regard I certainly respect and admire you most sincerely. But God has not yet willed or granted that you should be equal to the matter at present at issue between us. I say this, as I beg you to believe, in no spirit of arrogance, but I pray that the Lord may very soon make you as much superior to me in this matter as you are in all others. There is no novelty in it if God instructs Moses through Jethro*m* and teaches Paul through Ananias.*n* For as to your saying that you have wandered very far from the mark if you are ignorant of Christ, I think you yourself see what it implies. For it does not follow that everybody will go astray if you or I do. God is preached as being marvelous in God's saints, so that we may

---

*m*   Exodus 18.
*n*   Acts 9:10-19.

regard as saints those who are very far from sanctity. And it is not difficult to suppose that you, since you are human, may not have rightly understood or observed with due care the Scriptures or the sayings of the Teachers of the Early Church under whose guidance you think you are attaining your goal; and of this there is more than a hint in your statement that you are asserting nothing, but have only "discoursed." No one writes like that who has a thorough insight into the subject and rightly understands it. I for my part in this book *have not discoursed, but have asserted and do assert*, and I am unwilling to submit the matter to anyone's judgment, but advise everyone to yield assent. But may the Lord, whose cause this is, enlighten you and make you a vessel for honor and glory.

Amen.

# Image Credits